My Life in China and America

My Life in China and America

Yung Wing

MINT EDITIONS

My Life in China and America was first published in 1909.

This edition published by Mint Editions 2021.

ISBN 9781513278612 | E-ISBN 9781513279077

Published by Mint Editions®

 MINT
EDITIONS

minteditionbooks.com

Publishing Director: Jennifer Newens
Design & Production: Rachel Lopez Metzger
Project Manager: Micaela Clark
Typesetting: Westchester Publishing Services

Contents

I

BOYHOOD

I was born on the 17th of November, 1828, in the village of Nam Ping (South Screen) which is about four miles southwest of the Portuguese Colony of Macao, and is situated on Pedro Island lying west of Macao, from which it is separated by a channel of half a mile wide.

I was one of a family of four children. A brother was the eldest, a sister came next, I was the third, and another brother was the fourth and the youngest of the group. I am the only survivor of them all.

As early as 1834, an English lady, Mrs. Gutzlaff, wife of the Rev. Charles Gutzlaff, a missionary to China, came to Macao and, under the auspices of the Ladies' Association in London for the promotion of female education in India and the East, immediately took up the work of her mission by starting a girls' school for Chinese girls, which was soon followed by the opening of a school for boys also.

Mrs. Gutzlaff's comprador or factotum happened to come from the village I did and was, in fact, my father's friend and neighbor. It was through him that my parents heard about Mrs. Gutzlaff's school and it was doubtless through his influence and means that my father got me admitted into the school. It has always been a mystery to me why my parents should take it into their heads to put me into a foreign school, instead of a regular orthodox Confucian school, where my brother much older than myself was placed. Most assuredly such a step would have been more in play with Chinese public sentiment, taste, and the wants of the country at large, than to allow me to attend an English school; moreover, a Chinese cult is the only avenue in China that leads to political preferment, influence, power and wealth. I can only account for the departure thus taken on the theory that as foreign intercourse with China was just beginning to grow, my parents, anticipating that it might soon assume the proportions of a tidal wave, thought it worth while to take time by the forelock and put one of their sons to learning English that he might become one of the advanced interpreters and have a more advantageous position from which to make his way into the business and diplomatic world. This I take to be the chief aim that influenced my parents to put me into Mrs. Gutzlaff's Mission School.

As to what other results or sequences it has eventually brought about in my subsequent life, they were entirely left to Him who has control of all our devising and planning, as they are governed by a complete system of divine laws of antecedents and consequents, or of cause and effect.

In 1835, when I was barely seven years of age, my father took me to Macao. Upon reaching the school, I was brought before Mrs. Gutzlaff. She was the first English lady I had ever seen. On my untutored and unsophisticated mind she made a deep impression. If my memory serves me right, she was somewhat tall and well-built. She had prominent features which were strong and assertive; her eyes were of clear blue lustre, somewhat deep set. She had thin lips, supported by a square chin,—both indicative of firmness and authority. She had flaxen hair and eyebrows somewhat heavy. Her features taken collectively indicated great determination and will power.

As she came forward to welcome me in her long and full flowing white dress (the interview took place in the summer), surmounted by two large globe sleeves which were fashionable at the time and which lent her an exaggerated appearance, I remember most vividly I was no less puzzled than stunned. I actually trembled all over with fear at her imposing proportions—having never in my life seen such a peculiar and odd fashion. I clung to my father in fear. Her kindly expression and sympathetic smiles found little appreciative response at the outset, as I stood half dazed at her personality and my new environment. For really, a new world had dawned on me. After a time, when my homesickness was over and the novelty of my surroundings began gradually to wear away, she completely won me over through her kindness and sympathy. I began to look upon her more like a mother. She seemed to take a special interest in me; I suppose, because I was young and helpless, and away from my parents, besides being the youngest pupil in the school. She kept me among her girl pupils and did not allow me to mingle with what few boys there were at the time.

There is one escapade that I can never forget! It happened during the first year in the school, and was an attempt on my part to run away. I was shut up in the third story of the house, which had a wide open terrace on the top,—the only place where the girls and myself played and found recreation. We were not allowed to go out of doors to play in the streets. The boy pupils had their quarters on the ground floor and had full liberty to go out for exercise. I used to envy them their freedom and smuggled down stairs to mingle with them in their sports after school hours. I felt ill at ease to be shut up with the girls all alone way up in the third story. I wanted to see something of the outside world. I occasionally stole down stairs and ventured out to the wharves around which were clustered a number of small ferry boats which had a peculiar fascination to my young fancy. To gain my freedom, I planned to run away. The girls were all much older than I was, and a few sympathized with me in my wild scheme; doubtless, from the same restlessness of being too closely cooped up. I told them of my plan. Six of the older ones fell in with me in the idea. I was to slip out of the house alone, go down to the wharf and engage a covered boat to take us all in.

The next morning after our morning meal, and while Mrs. Gutzlaff was off taking her breakfast, we stole out unbeknown to any one and crowded into the boat and started off in hot haste for the opposite shore of Pedro Island. I was to take the whole party to my home and from there the girls were to disperse to their respective villages. We were half way across the channel when, to my great consternation, I saw a boat chasing us, making fast time and gaining on us all the while. No promise of additional pay was of any avail, because our two oars against their four made it impossible for us to win out; so our boatmen gave up the race at the waving of handkerchiefs in the other boat and the whole party was captured. Then came the punishment. We were marched through the whole school and placed in a row, standing on a long narrow school table placed at one end of the school room facing all the pupils in front of us. I was placed in the center of the row, with a tall foolscap mounted on my head, having three girls on the right and three on the left. I had pinned on my breast a large square placard bearing the inscription, "Head of the Runaways;" there we stood for a whole hour till school was dismissed. I never felt so humiliated in my life as I did when I was undergoing that ordeal. I felt completely crestfallen. Some of the mischievous fellows would extract a little fun out of this display by taking furtive glances and making wry faces at us. Mrs. Gutzlaff, in order to aggravate our punishment, had ordered ginger snaps and oranges to be distributed among the other pupils right before us.

Mrs. Gutzlaff's school, started in September, 1835, was originally for girls only. Pending the organization and opening of the so-called "Morrison Education Society School," in the interval between 1835 and 1839, a department for boys was temporarily incorporated into her school, and part of the subscription fund belonging to the M. E. S. School was devoted to the maintenance of this one.

This accounts for my entrance into Mrs. Gutzlaff's School, as one of only two boys first admitted. Her school being thus enlarged and modified temporarily, Mrs. Gutzlaff's two nieces—the Misses Parkes, sisters to Mr. Harry Parkes who was afterwards knighted, by reason of the conspicuous part he played in the second Opium War, in 1864, of which he was in fact the originator—came out to China as assistants in the school. I was fortunately placed under their instruction for a short time.

Afterwards the boys' school under Mrs. Gutzlaff and her two nieces, the Misses Parkes, was broken up; that event parted our ways in life in divergent directions. Mrs. Gutzlaff went over to the United States with three blind girls,—Laura, Lucy and Jessie. The Misses Parkes were married to missionaries, one to Dr. William Lockhart, a medical missionary; the other to a Rev. Mr. MacClatchy, also a missionary. They labored long in China, under the auspices of the London Missionary Society. The three blind girls whom Mrs. Gutzlaff took with her were taught by me to read on raised letters till they could read from the Bible and Pilgrim's Progress.

On my return to my home village I resumed my Chinese studies.

In the fall of 1840, while the Opium War was still going on, my father died, leaving four children on my mother's hands without means of support.

Fortunately, three of us were old enough to lend a helping hand. My brother was engaged in fishing, my sister helped in housework, and I took to hawking candy through my own village and the neighboring one. I took hold of the business in good earnest, rising at three o'clock every morning, and I did not come home until six o'clock in the evening. My daily earnings netted twenty-five cents, which I turned over to my mother, and with the help given by my brother, who was the main stay of the family, we managed to keep the wolf away from our door. I was engaged in hawking candy for about five months, and when winter was over, when no candy was made, I changed my occupation and went into the rice fields to glean rice after the reapers. My sister usually accompanied me in such excursions. But unlike Ruth of old, I had no Boaz to help me out when I was short in my gleaning. But my knowledge of English came to my rescue. My sister told the head reaper that I could speak, read and write English. This awakened the curiosity of the reaper. He beckoned me to him and asked me whether I wouldn't talk some "Red Hair Men" talk to him. He said he never heard of such talk in his life. I felt bashful and diffident at first, but my sister encouraged me and said "the reaper may give you a large bundle of rice sheaf to take home." This was said as a kind of prompter. The reaper was shrewd enough to take it up, and told me that if I would talk, he would give me a bundle heavier than I could carry. So I began and repeated the alphabet to him. All the reapers as well as the gleaners stood in vacant silence, with mouths wide open, grinning with evident delight. A few minutes after my maiden speech was delivered in the paddy field with water and mud almost knee deep, I was rewarded with several sheaves, and I had to hurry away in order to get two other boys to carry what my sister and I could not lug. Thus I came home loaded with joy and sheaves of golden rice to my mother, little dreaming that my smattering knowledge of English would serve me such a turn so early in my career. I was then about twelve years old. Even Ruth with her six measures of corn did not fare any better than I did.

Soon after the gleaning days, all too few, were over, a neighbor of mine who was a printer in the printing office of a Roman Catholic priest happened to be home from Macao on a vacation. He spoke to my mother about the priest wanting to hire a boy in his office who knew enough English to read the numerals correctly, so as to be able to fold and prepare the papers for the binders. My mother said I could do the work. So I was introduced to the priest and a bargain was struck. I returned home to report myself, and a few days later I was in Macao and entered upon my duty as a folder on a salary of $4.50 a month. My board and lodging came to $1.50—the balance of $3.00 was punctually sent to my mother every month. I did not get rich quickly in this employment, for I had been there but four months when a call for me to quit work came from a quarter I least expected. It had more the sound of heaven in it. It came from a Dr. Benjamin Hobson, a medical missionary in Macao whose hospital was not more than a mile from the printer's office. He sent word that he wanted to see me; that he had been hunting for me for months. I knew Dr. Hobson well, for I saw him a number of times at Mrs. Gutzlaff's. So I called on him. At the outset, I thought he was going to take me in to make a doctor of me, but no, he said he had a promise to fulfill. Mrs. Gutzlaff's last message to him, before she embarked for America with the three blind girls, was to be sure to find out where I was and to put me into the Morrison Education Society School as soon as it was opened for pupils.

"This is what I wanted to see you for," said Dr. Hobson. "Before you leave your employment and after you get the consent of your mother to let you go to the Morrison School, I would like to have you come to the hospital and stay with me for a short time so that I may become better acquainted with you, before I take you to the Morrison School, which is already opened for pupils, and introduce you to the teacher."

At the end of the interview, I went home to see my mother who, after some reluctance, gave her consent. I returned to Macao, bade farewell to the priest who, though reticent and reserved, not having said a word to me during all the four months I was in his employ, yet did not find fault with me in my work. I went over to the hospital. Dr. Hobson immediately set me to work with the mortar and pestle, preparing materials for ointments and pills. I used to carry a tray and accompany him in his rounds to visit the patients, in the benevolent work of alleviating their pains and sufferings. I was with him about a couple of months in the hospital work, at the end of which time he took me one day and introduced me to the Rev. Samuel Robins Brown, the teacher of the Morrison Education Society School.

II

School Days

The Morrison School was opened on the 1st of November, 1839, under the charge of the Rev. S. R. Brown who, with his wife, Mrs. Brown, landed at Macao on the 19th of February, 1839. Brown, who was afterwards made a D.D., was a graduate of Yale of the class of 1832. From his antecedents, he was eminently fitted to pioneer the first English school in China. I entered the school in 1841. I found that five other boys had entered ahead of me by one year. They were all studying primary arithmetic, geography, and reading. I had the start of them only in reading and pronouncing English well. We studied English in the forenoon, and Chinese in the afternoon. The names of the five boys were: 1. Wong Shing; 2. Li Kan; 3. Chow Wan; 4. Tong Chik; 5. Wong Foon. I made the sixth one and was the youngest of all. We formed the first class of the school, and became Brown's oldest pupils throughout, from first to last, till he left China in December, 1846, on account of poor health. Half of our original number accompanied him to this country, on his return.

The Morrison Education Society School came about in this way: Not long after the death of Dr. Robert Morrison, which occurred on the 1st of August, 1834, a circular was issued among the foreign residents on the 26th of January, 1835, calling for the formation of an Association to be named the "Morrison Education Society." Its object was to "improve and promote English education in China by schools and other means." It was called "Morrison" to commemorate the labors and works of that distinguished man who was sent out by the London Missionary Society as the first missionary to China in 1807. He crossed the Atlantic from London to New York where he embarked for China in the sailing vessel "Trident" on the 31st of January, 1807. He tried to land in Macao, but the jealousy of the Jesuits thwarted his purpose. He was obliged to go up to Canton. Finally, on account of the unsettled relations between the Chinese government and the foreign merchants there, he repaired to Malacca, and made that place the basis of his labors. He was the author of the first Anglo-Chinese dictionary, of three quarto volumes. He translated the Bible into Chinese; Leang Afah was his first Chinese convert and trained by him to preach. Leang afterwards became a powerful preacher. The importance and bearing of his dictionary and the translation of the Bible into Chinese, on subsequent missionary work in China, were fundamental and paramount. The preaching of his convert, Leang Afah, likewise contributed in no small degree towards opening up a new era in the religious life of China. His memory, therefore, is worthy of being kept alive by the establishment of a school named after him. Indeed, a university ought to have been permanently founded for that purpose instead of a school, whose existence was solely dependent upon the precarious and ephemeral subscriptions of transient foreign merchants in China.

At the close of the Opium War in 1840, and after the Island of Hong Kong had been ceded to the British government, the Morrison school was removed to Hong Kong in 1842. The site chosen for it was on the top of a hill about six hundred feet above the level of the sea. The hill is situated on the eastern end of Victoria Colony and was called "Morrison Hill" after the name of the school. It commands a fine view of the harbor, as that stretches from east to west. The harbor alone made Hong Kong the most coveted concession in Southern China. It is spacious and deep enough to hold the Navy of Great Britain, and it is that distinguishing feature and its strategic location that have made it what it is.

On the 12th of March, 1845, Mr. Wm. Allen Macy arrived in Hong Kong as an assistant teacher in the school. His arrival was timely, because the school, since its removal from Macao to Hong Kong, had been much enlarged. Three more classes of new pupils had been formed and the total number of pupils all told was more than forty. This was more than one man could manage. The assistant teacher was much needed. Brown continued his work in the school till the fall of 1846. Macy had a whole year in which to be broken into the work.

Between Brown and Macy there was a marked difference in temperament and character. Brown, on the one hand, showed evidences of a self-made man. He was cool in temperament, versatile in the adaptation of means to ends, gentlemanly and agreeable, and somewhat optimistic. He found no difficulty in endearing himself to his pupils, because he sympathized with them in their efforts to master their studies, and entered heart and soul into his work. He had an innate faculty of making things clear to the pupils and conveying to them his understanding of a subject without circumlocution, and with great directness and facility. This was owing in a great measure to his experience as a pedagogue, before coming out to China, and even before he entered college. He knew how to manage boys, because he knew boys' nature well, whether Chinese, Japanese or American. He impressed his pupils as being a fine teacher and one eminently fitted from inborn tact and temperament to be a successful school master, as he proved himself to be in his subsequent career in Auburn, N. Y., and in Japan.

Macy, the assistant teacher, was likewise a Yale man. He had never taught school before in his life, and had no occasion to do so. He possessed no previous experience to guide him in his new work of pedagogy in China. He was evidently well brought up and was a man of sensitive nature, and of fine moral sensibilities,—a soul full of earnestness and lofty ideals.

After the Morrison School was broken up in 1850, he returned to this country with his mother and took up theology in the Yale Theological Seminary. In 1854, he went back to China as a missionary under the American Board. I had graduated from Yale College then and was returning to China with him. We were the only passengers in that long, wearisome and most trying passage of 154 days from Sandy Hook to Hong Kong.

Brown left China in the winter of 1846. Four months before he left, he one day sprang a surprise upon the whole school. He told of his contemplated return to America on account of his health and the health of his family. Before closing his remarks by telling us of his deep interest in the school, he said he would like to take a few of his old pupils home with him to finish their education in the United States, and that those who wished to accompany him would signify it by rising. This announcement, together with his decision to return to America, cast a deep gloom over the whole school. A dead silence came over all of us. And then for several days afterwards the burden of our conversation was about Brown's leaving the school for good. The only cheerful ones among us were those who had decided to accompany him home. These were Wong Shing, Wong Foon and myself. When he requested those who wished to accompany him to the States to signify it by rising, I was the first one on my feet. Wong Foon was the second, followed by Wong Shing. But before regarding our cases as permanently settled, we were told to go home and ask the consent of our respective parents. My mother gave her consent with great reluctance, but after my earnest persuasion she yielded, though not without tears and sorrow. I consoled her with the fact that she had two more sons besides myself, and a daughter to look after her comfort. Besides, she was going to have a daughter-in-law to take care of her, as my elder brother was engaged to be married.

It may not be out of place to say that if it had depended on our own resources, we never could have come to America to finish our education, for we were all poor. Doubtless Brown must have had the project well discussed among the trustees of the school months before he broached the subject to his pupils.

It was also through his influence that due provision was made for the support of our parents for at least two years, during our absence in America. Our patrons who bore all our expenses did not intend that we should stay in this country longer than two years. They treated us nobly. They did a great work for us. Among those who bore a conspicuous part in defraying our expenses while in America, besides providing for the support of our aged parents, I can recall the names of Andrew Shortrede, proprietor and editor of the "Hong Kong China Mail" (he was a Scotchman, an old bachelor, and a noble and handsome specimen of humanity), A. A. Ritchie, an American merchant, and A. A. Campbell, another Scotchman. There were others unknown to me. The Olyphant Sons, David, Talbot and Robert, three brothers, leading merchants of New York, gave us a free passage from Hong Kong to New York in their sailing vessel, the "Huntress," which brought a cargo of tea at the same time. Though late in the day for me to mention the names of these benefactors who from pure motives of Christian philanthropy aided me in my education, yet it may be a source of satisfaction to their descendants, if there are any living in different parts of the world, to know that their sires took a prominent part in the education of the three Chinese youths,—Wong Shing, Wong Foon and myself.

III

Journey to America and First Experiences There

Being thus generously provided for, we embarked at Whompoa on the 4th of January, 1847, in the good ship "Huntress" under Captain Gillespie. As stated above, she belonged to the Olyphant Brothers and was loaded with a full cargo of tea. We had the northeast trade wind in our favor, which blew strong and steady all the way from Whompoa to St. Helena. There was no accident of any kind, excepting a gale as we doubled the Cape of Good Hope. The tops of the masts and ends of the yards were tipped with balls of electricity. The strong wind was howling and whistling behind us like a host of invisible Furies. The night was pitch dark and the electric balls dancing on the tips of the yards and tops of the masts, back and forth and from side to side like so many infernal lanterns in the black night, presented a spectacle never to be forgotten by me. I realized no danger, although the ship pitched and groaned, but enjoyed the wild and weird scene hugely. After the Cape was doubled, our vessel ploughed through the comparatively smooth waters of the Atlantic until we reached the Island of St. Helena where we were obliged to stop for fresh water and provisions. Most sailing vessels that were bound from the East for the Atlantic board were accustomed to make St. Helena their stopping place. St. Helena, as viewed from the shipboard, presented an outward appearance of a barren volcanic rock, as though freshly emerged from the baptism of fire and brimstone. Not a blade of grass could be seen on its burnt and charred surface. We landed at Jamestown, which is a small village in the valley of the Island. In this valley there was rich and beautiful vegetation. We found among the sparse inhabitants a few Chinese who were brought there by the East India Company's ships. They were middle-aged people, and had their families there. While there, we went over to Longwood where was Napoleon's empty tomb. A large weeping willow hung and swept over it. We cut a few twigs, and kept them alive till we reached this country and they were brought to Auburn, N. Y., by Mr. Brown, who planted them near his residence when he was teaching in the Auburn Academy for several years before his departure for Japan. These willows proved to be fine, handsome trees when I visited Auburn in 1854.

From St. Helena we took a northwesterly course and struck the Gulf Stream, which, with the wind still fair and favorable, carried us to New York in a short time. We landed in New York on the 12th of April, 1847, after a passage of ninety-eight days of unprecedented fair weather. The New York of 1847 was altogether a different city from the New York of 1909. It was a city of only 250,000 or 300,000 inhabitants; now it is a metropolis rivaling London in population, wealth and commerce. The whole of Manhattan Island is turned into a city of skyscrapers, churches and palatial residences.

Little did I realize when in 1845 I wrote, while in the Morrison School, a composition on "An Imaginary Voyage to New York and up the Hudson," that I was to see New York in reality. This incident leads me to the reflection that sometimes our imagination foreshadows what lies uppermost in our minds and brings possibilities within the sphere of realities. The Chinese Education Scheme is another example of the realities that came out of my day dreams a year before I graduated. So was my marrying an American wife. Still there are other day dreams yet to be realized; whether or no they will ever come to pass the future will determine.

Our stay in New York was brief. The first friends we had the good fortune to make in the new world, were Prof. David E. Bartlett and his wife. He was a professor in the New York Asylum for the Deaf and Dumb, and was afterwards connected with a like institution in Hartford. The Professor died in 1879. His wife, Mrs. Fanny P. Bartlett, survived him for nearly thirty years and passed away in the spring of 1907. She was a woman highly respected and beloved for her high Christian character and unceasing activities for good in the community in which she lived. Her influence was even extended to China by the few students who happened to enjoy her care and instruction. I count her as one of my most valued friends in America.

From New York we proceeded by boat to New Haven where we had an opportunity to see Yale College and were introduced to President Day. I had not then the remotest idea of becoming a graduate of one of the finest colleges of the country, as I did a few years afterwards. We went by rail from New Haven to Warehouse Point and from there to East Windsor, the home of Mrs. Elizabeth Brown, wife of Dr. Brown. Her parents were then living. Her father, the Rev. Shubael Bartlett, was the pastor of the East Windsor Congregational Church. I well remember the first Sabbath we attended his church. We three Chinese boys sat in the pastor's pew which was on the left of the pulpit, having a side view of the minister, but in full view of the whole congregation. We were the cynosure of the whole church. I doubt whether much attention was paid to the sermon that day.

The Rev. Shubael Bartlett was a genuine type of the old New England Puritan. He was exact and precise in all his manners and ways. He spoke in a deliberate and solemn tone, but full of sincerity and earnestness. He conducted himself as though he was treading on thin ice, cautiously and circumspectly. One would suppose from his appearance that he was austere and exacting, but he was gentle and thoughtful. He would have his family Bible and hymn book placed one on top of the other, squared and in straight lines, on the same spot on the table every morning for morning prayers. He always sat in the same spot for morning prayers. In other words, you always knew where to find him. His habits and daily life were as regular as clock work. I never heard him crack a joke or burst out in open laughter.

Mrs. Bartlett, Mrs. Brown's mother, was of a different makeup. She was always cheerful. A smile lighted up her features nearly all the time and for everyone she had a kind and cheerful word, while the sweet tone of her voice always carried with it cheerfulness and good will. Her genial temperament and her hospitality made the parsonage a favorite resort to all the friends and relatives of the family, who were quite numerous. It was always a puzzle to me how the old lady managed to make ends meet when her husband's salary was not over $400 a year. To be sure, the farm annually realized something, but Daniel, the youngest son, who was the staff of the old couple, had to work hard to keep up the prestige of the parsonage. It was in this parsonage that I found a temporary home while at school in Monson, and also in Yale.

IV

AT MONSON ACADEMY

We were in East Windsor for about a week; then we went up to Monson, Mass., to enter the Academy there. Monson Academy was, at one time, quite a noted preparatory school in New England, before high schools sprang into existence. Young men from all parts of the country were found here, undergoing preparation for colleges. It was its fortune, at different periods of its history, to have had men of character and experience for its principals. The Rev. Charles Hammond was one of them. He was in every sense a self-made man. He was a graduate of Yale; he was enthusiastically fond of the classics, and a great admirer of English literature. He was a man of liberal views and broad sympathies. He was well-known in New England as an educator and a champion of temperance and New England virtues. His high character gave the Academy a wide reputation and the school was never in a more prosperous condition than when he was principal. He took a special interest in us, the three Chinese students—Wong Shing, Wong Foon and myself—not so much from the novelty of having Chinese in the school as from his interest in China, and the possible good that might come out of our education.

In our first year in the Academy, we were placed in the English department. Greenleaf's Arithmetic, English Grammar, Physiology, and Upham's Mental Philosophy were our studies. In the last two studies we recited to the new preceptress, Miss Rebekah Brown, a graduate of Mt. Holyoke, the valedictorian of her class. She afterwards became the wife of Doctor A. S. McClean, of Springfield, Mass. She was a fine teacher and a woman of exceptional Christian virtues. She had an even and sweet temper, and was full of good will and good works. She and her husband, the good Doctor, took a genuine interest in me; they gave me a home during some of my college vacations, and helped me in various ways in my struggle through Yale. I kept up my correspondence with them after my return to China, and upon my coming back to this country, I was always cordially invited to their home in Springfield. It was on account of such a genuine friendship that I made Springfield my headquarters in 1872, when I brought the first installment of Government students to this country.

Brown placed us under the care of his mother, Mrs. Phoebe H. Brown. We boarded with her, but had a separate room assigned us in a dwelling right across the road, opposite to her cottage. Her widowed daughter with her three boys had taken up all the spare rooms in the cottage, which accounts for the want of accommodation for us.

In those primitive days, board and lodging in the country were very reasonable. Indigent students had a fair chance to work their way for an education. I remember we paid for board and lodging, including fuel, light and washing, only $1.25 a week for each, but we had to take care of our own rooms and, in the winter, saw and split our own wood, which we found to be capital exercise.

Our lodging was about half a mile from the academy. We had to walk three times a day to school and back, in the dead of winter when the snow was three feet deep; that gave us plenty of exercise, keen appetites and kept us in fine condition.

I look back upon my acquaintance with Mrs. Phoebe H. Brown with a mingled feeling of respect and admiration. She certainly was a remarkable New England woman—a woman of surpassing strength of moral and religious character. Those who have had the rare privilege of reading her stirring biography, will, I am sure, bear me out in this statement. She went through the crucible of unprecedented adversities and trials of life and came out one of the rare shining lights that beautify the New England sky. She is the authoress of the well-known hymn, "I love to steal awhile away from every cumbering care," etc., which breathes the calm spirit of contentment and resignation wherever sung.

The Rev. Charles Hammond, the principal of the academy when we joined it, was a graduate of Yale, as I stated before, and a man of a fine cultivated taste. He was an enthusiastic admirer of Shakespeare, who was his favorite poet; among orators, he was partial to Daniel Webster. He had the faculty of inspiring his pupils with the love of the beautiful, both in ancient and modern literature. In our daily recitations, he laid a greater stress on pointing out the beauties of a sentence and its construction, than he did on grammatical rules, moods and tenses. He was a fine writer. His addresses and sermons were pointed and full of life. Like Dr. Arnold of Rugby, he aimed to build character in his pupils and not to convert them into walking encyclopedias, or intelligent parrots. It was through him that I was introduced to Addison, Goldsmith, Dickens, Sir Walter Scott, the Edinburgh Reviews, Macaulay and Shakespeare, which formed the bulk of my reading while in Monson.

During my first year in the Monson Academy, I had no idea of taking a collegiate course. It was well understood that I was to return to China at the end of 1849, and the appropriation was made to suit such a plan. In the fall of 1848, after Wong Shing—the eldest of the three of us—had returned to China on account of his poor health, Wong Foon and myself, who were left behind to continue our studies for another year, frequently met to talk over future plans for the end of the prescribed time. We both decided finally to stay in this country to continue our studies, but the question arose, who was going to back us financially after 1849? This was the Gordian Knot. We concluded to consult Mr. Hammond and Mr. Brown on the subject. They both decided to have the matter referred to our patrons in Hong Kong. Reply came that if we wished to prosecute our studies after 1849, they would be willing to continue their support through a professional course, if we were willing to go over to Scotland to go through the University of Edinburgh. This was a generous and noble-hearted proposal.

Wong Foon, on his part, after much deliberation, decided to accept the offer and go over to Scotland at the end of 1849, while, on my part, I preferred to remain in this country to continue my studies here with the view of going to Yale. Wong Foon's decision had relieved him of all financial anxieties, while the problem of how I was to pay my education bills after 1849, still remained to be solved. But I did not allow the perplexities of the future to disturb my peace of mind. I threw all my anxieties to the wind, trusting to a wise Providence to care for my future, as it had done for my past.

Wong Foon and I, having taken our decisive steps, dropped our English studies at the close of the school year of 1849, and in the fall of the same year we began the A B C's of our classical course. In the summer of 1850, we graduated from the academy. Wong Foon, by previous arrangements, went over to Scotland and entered the University of Edinburgh. I remained in this country and finally entered Yale. It was fully a decade since we had met for the first time in the Morrison School in Macao, in 1840, to become school-mates as well as class-mates. Now that link was broken.

Wong was in the University seven years. After completing his professional studies as a doctor, he returned to China in 1857. He was a fine scholar. He graduated the third man in his medical class. He also distinguished himself in his profession. His ability and skill secured for him an enviable reputation as one of the ablest surgeons east of the Cape of Good Hope at that time. He had a fine practice in Canton, where the foreign residents retained him as their physician in preference to European doctors. He was very successful and made quite a fortune before his death, which took place in 1879. Both the native and foreign communities felt his loss. He was highly respected and honored by Chinese and foreigners for his Christian character and the purity of his life.

V

My College Days

Before entering Yale, I had not solved the problem of how I was to be carried through the collegiate course without financial backing of a definite and well-assured character. It was an easy matter to talk about getting an education by working for it, and there is a kind of romance in it that captivates the imagination, but it is altogether a different thing to face it in a business and practical way. So it proved to me, after I had put my foot into it. I had no one except Brown, who had already done so much for me in bringing me to this country, and Hammond, who fitted me for college. To them I appealed for advice and counsel. I was advised to avail myself of the contingent fund provided for indigent students. It was in the hands of the trustees of the academy and so well guarded that it could not be appropriated without the recipient's signing a written pledge that he would study for the ministry and afterwards become a missionary. Such being the case, I made up my mind that it would be utterly useless for me to apply for the fund. However, a day was appointed for me to meet the trustees in the parsonage, to talk over the subject. They said they would be too glad to have me avail myself of the fund, provided I was willing to sign a pledge that after graduation I should go back to China as a missionary. I gave the trustees to understand that I would never give such a pledge for the following reasons: First, it would handicap and circumscribe my usefulness. I wanted the utmost freedom of action to avail myself of every opportunity to do the greatest good in China. If necessary, I might be obliged to create new conditions, if I found old ones were not favorable to any plan I might have for promoting her highest welfare.

In the second place, the calling of a missionary is not the only sphere in life where one can do the most good in China or elsewhere. In such a vast empire, there can be hardly any limit put upon one's ambition to do good, if one is possessed of the Christ-spirit; on the other hand, if one has not such a spirit, no pledge in the world could melt his ice-bound soul.

In the third place, a pledge of that character would prevent me from taking advantage of any circumstance or event that might arise in the life of a nation like China, to do her a great service.

"For these reasons," I said, "I must decline to give the pledge and at the same time decline to accept your kind offer to help me. I thank you, gentlemen, very much, for your good wishes."

Both Brown and Hammond afterwards agreed that I took the right view on the subject and sustained me in my position. To be sure, I was poor, but I would not allow my poverty to gain the upper hand and compel me to barter away my inward convictions of duty for a temporary mess of pottage.

During the summer of 1850, it seems that Brown who had been making a visit in the South to see his sister, while there had occasion to call on some of the members of "The Ladies' Association" in Savannah, Ga., to whom he mentioned my case. He returned home in the nick of time, just after I had the interview with the board of trustees of the academy. I told him of the outcome, when, as stated above, he approved of my position, and told me what he had done. He said that the members of the association agreed to help me in college. On the strength of that I gathered fresh courage, and went down to New Haven to pass my examination for entrance. How I got in, I do not know, as I had had only fifteen months of Latin and twelve months of Greek, and ten months of mathematics. My preparation had been interrupted because the academy had been broken up by the Palmer & New London R.R. that was being built close by. As compared with the college preparations of nine-tenths of my class-mates, I was far behind. However, I passed without condition. But I was convinced I was not sufficiently prepared, as my recitations in the class-room clearly proved. Between the struggle of how to make ends meet financially and how to keep up with the class in my studies, I had a pretty tough time of it. I used to sweat over my studies till twelve o'clock every night the whole Freshman year. I took little or no exercise and my health and strength began to fail and I was obliged to ask for a leave of absence of a week. I went to East Windsor to get rested and came back refreshed.

In the Sophomore year, from my utter aversion to mathematics, especially to differential and integral calculus, which I abhorred and detested, and which did me little or no good in the way of mental discipline, I used to fizzle and flunk so often that I really thought I was going to be dropped from the class, or dismissed from college. But for some unexplained reasons I was saved from such a catastrophe, and I squeezed through the second year in college with so low a mark that I was afraid to ask my division tutor, who happened to be Tutor

Blodget, who had me in Greek, about it. The only redeeming feature that saved me as a student in the class of 1854, was the fortunate circumstance that I happened to be a successful competitor on two occasions in English composition in my division. I was awarded the first prize in the second term, and the first prize in the third term of the year. These prizes gave me quite an éclat in the college as well as in the outside world, but I was not at all elated over them on account of my poor scholarship which I felt keenly through the whole college course.

Before the close of my second year, I succeeded in securing the stewardship of a boarding club consisting of sophomores and juniors. There were altogether twenty members. I did all the marketing and served at the table. In this way, I earned my board through the latter half of my college course. In money matters, I was supplied with remittances from "The Ladies' Association" in Savannah, and also contributions from the Olyphant Brothers of New York. In addition to these sources of supply, I was paid for being an assistant librarian to the "Brothers in Unity," which was one of the two college debating societies that owned a library, and of which I was a member.

In my senior year I was again elected librarian to the same Society and got $30.00. These combined sums were large enough to meet all my cash bills, since my wants had to be finely trimmed to suit the cloth. If most of the country parsons of that period could get along with a salary of $200 or $300 a year (supplemented, of course, with an annual donation party, which sometimes carried away more than it donated), having as a general thing a large family to look after, I certainly ought to have been able to get through college with gifts of nearly a like amount, supplemented with donations of shirts and stockings from ladies who took an interest in my education.

The class of 1854, to which I had the honor and the good fortune to belong, graduated ninety-eight all told. Being the first Chinaman who had ever been known to go through a first-class American college, I naturally attracted considerable attention; and from the fact that I was librarian for one of the college debating societies (Linonia was the other) for two years, I was known by members of the three classes above, and members of the three classes below me. This fact had contributed toward familiarizing me with the college world at large, and my nationality, of course, added piquancy to my popularity.

As an undergraduate, I had already acquired a factitious reputation within the walls of Yale. But that was ephemeral and soon passed out of existence after graduation.

All through my college course, especially in the closing year, the lamentable condition of China was before my mind constantly and weighed on my spirits. In my despondency, I often wished I had never been educated, as education had unmistakably enlarged my mental and moral horizon, and revealed to me responsibilities which the sealed eye of ignorance can never see, and sufferings and wrongs of humanity to which an uncultivated and callous nature can never be made sensitive. The more one knows, the more he suffers and is consequently less happy; the less one knows, the less he suffers, and hence is more happy. But this is a low view of life, a cowardly feeling and unworthy of a being bearing the impress of divinity. I had started out to get an education. By dint of hard work and self-denial I had finally secured the coveted prize and although it might not be so complete and symmetrical a thing as could be desired, yet I had come right up to the conventional standard and idea of a liberal education. I could, therefore, call myself an educated man and, as such, it behooved me to ask, "What am I going to do with my education?" Before the close of my last year in college I had already sketched out what I should do. I was determined that the rising generation of China should enjoy the same educational advantages that I had enjoyed; that through western education China might be regenerated, become enlightened and powerful. To accomplish that object became the guiding star of my ambition. Towards such a goal, I directed all my mental resources and energy. Through thick and thin, and the vicissitudes of a checkered life from 1854 to 1872, I labored and waited for its consummation.

VI

RETURN TO CHINA

In entering upon my life's work which to me was so full of meaning and earnestness, the first episode was a voyage back to the old country, which I had not seen for nearly ten years, but which had never escaped my mind's eye nor my heart's yearning for her welfare. I wanted very much to stay a few years longer in order to take a scientific course. I had taken up surveying in the Sheffield Scientific School just as that department was starting into existence under Professor Norton. Had I had the means to prosecute a practical profession, that might have helped to shorten and facilitate the way to the goal I had in view; but as I was poor and my friends thought that a longer stay in this country might keep me here for good, and China would lose me altogether, I was for this and other reasons induced to return. The scientific course was accordingly abandoned. The persons who were most interested in my return to China were Pelatiah Perit of Messrs. Goodhue & Co., merchants in the China trade, and the Olyphant Brothers, who had taken such a lively interest eight years before in helping me to come over in their ship, the "Huntress." These gentlemen had no other motive in desiring me to return to China than that of hoping to see me useful in Christianizing the Chinese, which was in harmony with their well-known broad and benevolent characters.

On the 13th of November, 1854, the Rev. William Allen Macy, who went out to Hong Kong to take the place of the Rev. Dr. Brown, as teacher in the Morrison Education Society School in 1845, went back to China as a missionary under the American Board, and we were fellow-passengers on board the sailing clipper ship "Eureka," under Captain Whipple, of Messrs. Chamber, Heisser & Co., of New York.

Winter is the worst season of the year to go on an eastern voyage in a sailing vessel, via the Cape of Good Hope. The northeast trade winds prevail then and one is sure to have head winds all the way. The "Eureka," in which Macy and myself were the only passengers, took that route to Hong Kong. We embarked on board of her as she rode in midstream of the East River. The day was bleak and bitingly cold. No handkerchiefs were fluttering in the air, waving a good voyage; no sound from the shore cheered us as the anchor was weighed, and as the tug towed us out as far as Sandy Hook. There we were left to our own resources. The sails were not furled to their full extent, but were reefed for tacking, as the wind was nearly dead ahead and quite strong. We found the "Eureka" to be empty of cargo, and empty even of ballast of any kind; for that reason she acted like a sailor who had just had his nip before he went out to sea. She tossed up and down and twisted from right to left, just as though she had a little too much to keep her balance. It was in such a fashion that she reeled her way from Sandy Hook to Hong Kong—a distance of nearly 13,000 nautical miles, which took her 154 days to accomplish. It was decidedly the most uninteresting and wearisome voyage I ever took in my life. The skipper was a Philadelphian. He had the unfortunate habit of stuttering badly, which tended to irritate a temper naturally quick and fiery. He was certainly a ludicrous object to look at. It was particularly in the morning that he might be seen pacing the quarter deck, scanning the sky. This, by the spectator, was deemed necessary for the skipper to work himself up to the right pitch, preliminary to his pantomimic performances in his battle with the head wind. All at once, he halted, stared at the quarter of the sky from whence the malicious head wind came. With a face all bloated and reddened by intense excitement, his eyes almost standing out of their sockets, and all ablaze with uncontrollable rage, with arms uplifted, he would clutch his hair as if plucking it out by the roots, gnash his teeth, and simultaneously he would jump up and down, stamping on the deck, and swear at the Almighty for sending him head winds. The air for the moment was split with his revolting imprecations and blasphemous oaths that were exclaimed through the laborious process of stammering and stuttering, which made him a most pitiable object to behold. In the early part of the voyage it was a painful sight to see him working himself up to that pitch of contortion and paroxysm of rage which made him appear more like an insane than a sane man, but as these exhibitions were of daily occurrence for the greater part of the voyage, we came to regard him as no longer deserving of sympathy and pity, but rather with contempt. After his passion had spent its force, and he subsided into his calmer and normal mood, he would drop limply into a cane chair, where he would sit for hours all by himself. For the sake of diversion, he would rub his hands together, and soliloquize quietly to himself, an occasional smile breaking over his face, which made him look like an innocent idiot. Before the voyage was half through, the skipper had made such a fool of himself through his silly and insane conduct about the wind, that he became the laughing stock of the whole crew, who, of course, did not dare to show any outward signs of insubordination. The sailing of the vessel was entirely in the hands of the first mate, who was literally a sea-tyrant. The crew was composed of Swedes and Norwegians. If it had been made up of Americans, the inhuman treatment by the officers might have driven them to desperate extremities, because the men were over-worked night and day in incessant tacking. The only time that they found a resting spell was when the ship was becalmed in the tropics when not a breath of wind was to be had for several days at a time. Referring to my diary kept in that memorable voyage,—it took us nearly two weeks to beat up the Macassar straits. This event tried our patience sorely. After it was passed, the skipper made the remark within the hearing of the Rev. Macy that the reason he had bad luck was because he had a Jonah on board. My friend Macy took the remark in a good-natured way and gave me a significant smile. We were just then discussing the feat of going through the Macassar straits and I remarked in a tone just loud enough to be heard by the old skipper that if I had charge of the vessel, I could take her through in less than ten days. This was meant as a direct reflection on the poor seamanship of the old fellow (for he really was a miserable sailor), as well as to serve as a retaliation for what he said a few minutes before, that there was a Jonah on board.

In the dead of winter, the passage to the East should have been taken around Cape Horn instead of the Cape of Good Hope, in which case we would no doubt have had strong and fair wind all the way from New York to Hong Kong, which would not only have shortened the voyage but also saved the captain a world of swearing and an incalculable amount of wear and tear on his nervous system. But as a passenger only, I had no idea of the financial motive back of the move to send the ship off perfectly empty and unballasted, right in the teeth of the northeast monsoon. I would have been glad to go around Cape Horn, as that would have added a new route to my journeying around the world, and furnished me with new incidents as well.

As we approached Hong Kong, a Chinese pilot boarded us. The captain wanted me to ask him whether there were any dangerous rocks and shoals nearby. I could not for the life of me recall my Chinese in order to interpret for him; the pilot himself understood English, and he was the first Chinese teacher to give me the terms in Chinese for dangerous rocks and shoals. So the skipper and Macy, and a few other persons who were present at the time, had the laugh on me, who, being a Chinese, yet was not able to speak the language.

My first thought upon landing was to walk up to the office of the "China Mail," to pay my respects to Andrew Shortrede, the proprietor and editor of the paper, and the friend who supported me for over a year, while I was in Monson Academy. After seeing him and accepting his hospitality by way of an invitation to take up my quarters in his house, I lost no time in hastening over to Macao to see my aged and beloved mother, who, I knew, yearned to see her long-absent boy. Our meeting was arranged a day beforehand. I was in citizen's dress and could not conveniently change the same for my Chinese costume. I had also allowed a pair of mustaches to grow, which, according to Chinese custom, was not becoming for an unmarried young man to do. We met with tears of joy, gratitude and thanksgiving. Our hearts were too full even to speak at first. We gave way to our emotions. As soon as we were fairly composed, she began to stroke me all over, as expressive of her maternal endearment which had been held in patient suspense for at least ten years. As we sat close to each other, I gave her a brief recital of my life in America, for I knew she would be deeply interested in the account. I told her that I had just finished a long and wearisome voyage of five months' duration, but had met with no danger of any kind; that during my eight years of sojourn in the United States, I was very kindly treated by the good people everywhere; that I had had good health and never been seriously sick, and that my chief object during the eight years was to study and prepare myself for my life work in China. I explained to her that I had to go through a preparatory school before entering college; that the college I entered was Yale—one of the leading colleges of the United States, and that the course was four years, which accounted for my long stay and delayed my return to China. I told her that at the end of four years I had graduated with the degree of A.B.,—analogous to the Chinese title of Siu Tsai, which is interpreted "Elegant Talent;" that it was inscribed on a parchment of sheep skin and that to graduate from Yale College was considered a great honor, even to a native American, and much more so to a Chinese. She asked me näively how much money it conferred. I said it did not confer any money at once, but it enabled one to make money quicker and easier than one can who has not been educated; that it gave one greater influence and power among men and if he built on his college education, he would be more likely to become the leader of men, especially if he had a well-established character. I told her my college education was worth more to me than money, and that I was confident of making plenty of money.

"Knowledge," I said, "is power, and power is greater than riches. I am the first Chinese to graduate from Yale College, and that being the case, you have the honor of being the first and only mother out of the countless millions of mothers in China at this time, who can claim the honor of having a son who is the first Chinese graduate of a first-class American college. Such an honor is a rare thing to possess." I also assured her that as long as I lived all her comforts and wants would be scrupulously and sedulously looked after, and that nothing would be neglected to make her contented and happy. This interview seemed to give her great comfort and satisfaction. She seemed very happy over it. After it was ended, she looked at me with a significant smile and said, "I see you have already raised your mustaches. You know you have a brother who is much older than you are; he hasn't grown his mustaches yet. You must have yours off." I promptly obeyed her mandate, and as I entered the room with a clean face, she smiled with intense satisfaction, evidently thinking that with all my foreign education, I had not lost my early training of being obedient to my mother. And if she could only have read my heart, she would have found how every throb palpitated with the most tender love for her. During the remaining years of her life, I had the rare privilege of seeing her often and ministered to her every comfort that it was in my power to bestow. She passed away in 1858, at the age of sixty-four, twenty-four years after the death of my father. I was in Shanghai at the time of her death. I returned to my native village in time to attend her funeral.

In the summer of 1855, I took up my residence in Canton, with the Rev. Mr. Vrooman, a missionary under the American Board. His headquarters were in Ham Ha Lan, in the vicinity of the government execution ground, which is in the southwestern outskirts of the city, close to the bank of the Pearl River. While there, I began my Chinese studies and commenced to regain the dialect of Canton, which I had forgotten during my stay in the United States. In less than six months, the language came back to me readily, although I was still a little rusty in it. I was also making slow progress in recovering the written language, in which I was not well-grounded before leaving China, in 1846. I had studied it only four years, which was considered a short time in which to master the written language. There is a greater difference between the written and the spoken language of China than there is between the written and spoken English language. The Chinese written language is stilted and full of conventional forms. It is understood throughout the whole empire, but differently pronounced in different provinces and localities. The spoken language is cut up into endless dialects and in certain provinces like Fuhkien, Anhui and Kiangsu, the people are as foreigners to each other in the matter of dialects. Such are the peculiar characteristics of the ideographic and spoken languages of China.

During the six months of my residence in Canton, while trying to recover both the written and spoken languages, Kwang Tung province was thrown into a somewhat disorganized condition. The people of Canton attempted to raise a provincial insurrection or rebellion entirely distinct from the Taiping rebellion which was being carried on in the interior of China with marked success. To suppress and nip it in the bud, drastic measures were resorted to by Viceroy Yeh Ming Hsin, who, in the summer of 1855, decapitated seventy-five thousand people, most of whom, I was told, were innocent. My residence was within half a mile of the execution ground, as stated above, and one day, out of curiosity, I ventured to walk over to the place. But, oh! what a sight. The ground was perfectly drenched with human blood. On both sides of the driveway were to be seen headless human trunks, piled up in heaps, waiting to be taken away for burial. But no provision had been made to facilitate their removal.

The execution was carried on on a larger scale than had been expected, and no provision had been made to find a place large enough to bury all the bodies. There they were, left exposed to a burning sun. The temperature stood from morning to night in midsummer steadily at 90° Fahrenheit, and sometimes higher. The atmosphere within a radius of two thousand yards of the execution ground was heavily charged with the poisonous and pestilential vapor that was reeking from the ground already over-saturated with blood and from the heaps of corpses which had been left behind for at least two days, and which showed signs of rapid decomposition. It was a wonder to me that no virulent epidemic had sprung up from such an infectious spot to decimate the compact population of the city of Canton. It was a fortunate circumstance that at last a deep and extensive ravine, located in the far-off outskirts of the western part of the city, was found, which was at once converted into a sepulchral receptacle into which this vast human hecatomb was dumped. It was said that no earth was needed to be thrown over these corpses to cover them up; the work was accomplished by countless swarms of worms of a reddish hue and of an appearance that was perfectly hideous and revolting.

I was told that during the months of June, July and August, of 1855, seventy-five thousand people had been decapitated; that more than half of that number were declared to be innocent of the charge of rebellion, but that the accusation was made as a pretext to exact money from them. This wholesale slaughter, unparalleled in the annals of modern civilization, eclipsing even the enormities and blood-thirstiness of Caligula and Nero, or even the French Revolution, was perpetrated by Yeh Ming Hsin, who was appointed viceroy of Kwang Tung and Kwangsi in 1854.

Yeh Ming Hsin was a native of Han-Yang. Han-Yang is a part of the port of Hankau, and was destroyed with it when the Taiping rebels took possession of it. It was said that Yeh Ming Hsin had immense estates in Han-Yang, which were completely destroyed by fire. This circumstance embittered him towards the Taiping rebels and as the Taiping leaders hailed from Kwang Tung and Kwangsi, he naturally transferred his hatred to the people of those two provinces. It was in the lofty position of a viceroy that he found his opportunity to wreak his private and personal vengeance upon the Canton people. This accounts for his indiscriminate slaughter of them, and for the fact that he did not deign to give them even the semblance of a trial, but hurried them from life to death like packs of cattle to the shambles.

But this human monster did not dream that his day of reckoning was fast approaching. Several years after this appalling sacrifice of human life, in 1855, he got into trouble with the British government. He was captured by the British forces and banished to some obscure and remote corner in India where he led a most ignominious life, hated by the whole Chinese nation, and despised by the world at large.

On my return to headquarters, after my visit to the execution ground, I felt faint-hearted and depressed in spirit. I had no appetite for food, and when night came, I was too nervous for sleep. The scene I had looked upon during the day had stirred me up. I thought then that the Taiping rebels had ample grounds to justify their attempt to overthrow the Manchu régime. My sympathies were thoroughly enlisted in their favor and I thought seriously of making preparations to join the Taiping rebels, but upon a calmer reflection, I fell back on the original plan of doing my best to recover the Chinese language as fast as I possibly could and of following the logical course of things, in order to accomplish the object I had at heart.

VII

EFFORT TO FIND A POSITION

Having at last succeeded in mastering the spoken language sufficiently to speak it quite fluently, I at once set to work to find a position in which I could not only support myself and mother, but also form a plan for working out my ideas of reform in China.

Doctor Peter Parker, who had been a medical missionary under the American Board for many years in Canton, was at that time made United States Commissioner as a temporary expedient, to take the place of an accredited minister plenipotentiary—a diplomatic appointment not yet come into existence, because the question of a foreign minister resident in Peking was still under negotiation, and had not been fully settled as a permanent diplomatic arrangement between the Peking government and the Treaty Powers. Dr. Parker was given the appointment of commissioner on account of his long residence in China and his ability to speak the Chinese language, but not on account of any special training as a diplomat, nor for legal knowledge. It was through Mr. M. N. Hitchcock, an American merchant of the firm of Messrs. King & Co., and a mutual friend of Dr. Parker and myself, that I became the Doctor's private secretary. I knew Dr. Parker while I was at Mrs. Gutzlaff's School, and he doubtless knew I had recently graduated from Yale, which was his Alma Mater also. His headquarters were in Canton, but he spent his summers in Macao. I was with him only three months. My salary was $15 a month (not large enough to spoil me at any rate). He had very little for me to do, but I thought that by being identified with him, I might possibly come in contact with Chinese officials. However, this was far from being the case. Seeing that I could neither learn anything from him, nor enlarge my acquaintance with the Chinese officials, I gave up my position as his secretary and went over to Hong Kong to try to study law. Through my old friend, Andrew Shortrede, who generously extended to me the hospitality of his house, I succeeded in securing the position of the interpretership in the Hong Kong Supreme Court. The situation paid me $75 a month. Having this to fall back upon, I felt encouraged to go ahead in my effort to study law. Accordingly, I was advised to apprentice myself to an attorney or solicitor-at-law. In the

English court of practice, it seems that there are two distinct classes of lawyers—attorneys or solicitors, and barristers. The first prepares in writing all evidences, facts, and proofs of a case, hands them to the barrister or counsel, who argues the case in court according to law.

I apprenticed myself to an attorney, who was recommended to me by my old patron and friend, Shortrede. I was not aware that by going into the British Colony in Hong Kong to become an attorney, I was stepping on the toes of the British legal fraternity, nor that by apprenticing myself to an attorney instead of to the new attorney-general of the Colony, who, without my knowledge, wanted me himself, I had committed another mistake, which eventually necessitated my leaving Hong Kong altogether.

First of all, all the attorneys banded themselves together against me, because, as they openly stated in all the local papers except the "China Mail," if I were allowed to practice my profession, they might as well pack up and go back to England, for as I had a complete knowledge of both English and Chinese I would eventually monopolize all the Chinese legal business. So they made it too hot for me to continue in my studies.

In the next place, I was not aware that the attorney-general wanted me to apprentice myself to him, for he did all he could in his capacity as attorney-general of the Colony to use his influence to open the way for me to become an attorney, by draughting a special colonial ordinance to admit Chinese to practice in the Hong Kong Colony as soon as I could pass my examinations. This ordinance was sent to the British government to be sanctioned by Parliament before it became valid and a colonial law. It was sanctioned and thus became a colonial ordinance.

In the meanwhile, Anstey, the attorney-general, found out that I had already apprenticed myself to Parson, the attorney. From that time forth I had no peace. I was between two fires—the batteries operated by the attorneys opened on me with redoubled energy, and the new battery, operated by the attorney-general, opened its fire. He found fault with my interpreting, which he had never done previously. Mr. Parson saw how things stood. He himself was also under a hot fire from both sides. So in order to save himself, he told me plainly and candidly that he had to give me up and made the article of apprenticeship between us null and void. I, on my part, had to give up my position as interpreter in the Supreme Court. Parson, himself, not long after I had abandoned my apprenticeship and my position as interpreter, for reasons satisfactory to himself, gave up his business in Hong Kong and returned to England. So master and pupil left their posts at pretty nearly the same time.

A retrospective view of my short experience in Hong Kong convinced me that it was after all the best thing that I did not succeed in becoming a lawyer in Hong Kong, as the theatre of action there would have been too restricted and circumscribed. I could not have come in touch with the leading minds of China, had I been bound up in that rocky and barren Colony. Doubtless I might have made a fortune if I had succeeded in my legal profession, but as circumstances forced me to leave the Colony, my mind was directed northward to Shanghai, and in August, 1856, I left Hong Kong in the tea clipper, "Florence," under Captain Dumaresque, of Boston. He was altogether a different type of man from the captain of the "Eureka" which brought me out in 1855. He was kind, intelligent and gentlemanly. When he found out who I was, he offered me a free passage from Hong Kong to Shanghai. He was, in fact, the sole owner of the vessel, which was named after his daughter, Florence. The passage was a short one—lasting only seven days—but before it was over, we became great friends.

Not long after my arrival in Shanghai, I found a situation in the Imperial Customs Translating Department, at a salary of Tls. 75 a month, equivalent to $100 Mexican. For want of a Chinese silver currency the Mexican dollar was adopted. This was one point better than the interpretership in the Hong Kong Supreme Court. The duties were not arduous and trying. In fact, they were too simple and easy to suit my taste and ambition. I had plenty of time to read. Before three months of trial in my new situation, I found that things were not as they should be, and if I wished to keep a clean and clear record and an untarnished character, I could not remain long in the service. Between the interpreters who had been in the service many years and the Chinese shippers there existed a regular system of graft. After learning this, and not wishing to be implicated with the others in the division of the spoils in any way or shape, I made up my mind to resign. So one day I called upon the Chief Commissioner of Customs, ostensibly to find out what my future prospects were in connection with the Customs Service—whether or not there were any prospects of my being promoted to the position of a commissioner. I was told that no such prospects were held out to me or to any other Chinese interpreter. I, therefore, at once decided to throw up my position. So I sent in my resignation, which was at first not accepted. A few days after my first interview, Lay, the chief commissioner, strenuously tried to persuade me to change my mind, and offered as an inducement to raise my salary to Tls. 200 a month, evidently thinking that I was only bluffing in order to get higher wages. It did not occur to him that there was at least one Chinaman who valued a clean reputation and an honest character more than money; that being an educated man, I saw no reason why I should not be given the same chances to rise in the service of the Chinese government as an Englishman, nor why my individuality should not be recognized and respected in every walk of life. He little thought that I had aspirations even higher than his, and that I did not care to associate myself with a pack of Custom-house interpreters and inspectors, who were known to take bribes; that a man who expects others to respect him, must first respect himself. Such were my promptings. I did not state the real cause of my quitting the service, but at the end of four months' trial I left the service in order to try my fortune in new fields more congenial.

My friends at the time looked upon me as a crank in throwing up a position yielding me Tls. 200 a month for something uncertain and untried. This in their estimation was the height of folly. They little realized what I was driving at. I had a clean record and I meant to keep it clean. I was perfectly aware that in less than a year since my return to China, I had made three shifts. I myself began to think I was too mercurial to accomplish anything substantial, or that I was too dreamy to be practical or too proud to succeed in life. But in a strenuous life one needs to be a dreamer in order to accomplish possibilities. We are not called into being simply to drudge for an animal existence. I had had to work hard for my education, and I felt that I ought to make the most of what little I had, not so much to benefit myself individually as to make it a blessing common to my race. By these shifts and changes I was only trying to find my true bearing, and how I could make myself a blessing to China.

VIII

Experiences in Business

The next turn I took, after leaving the Imperial Customs, was clerk in an English house—tea and silk merchants. During the few months that I was with them, I gained quite an insight into mercantile business, and the methods of conducting it, which proved to be profitable knowledge and experience to me later on. Six months after I had entered upon my new sphere as a make-shift, the firm dissolved partnership, which once more threw me out of a position, and I was again cast upon the sea of uncertainty. But during my connection with the firm, two little incidents occurred which I must not fail to relate.

One Thursday evening, as I was returning home from a prayer meeting held in the Union Chapel in Shanghai, I saw ahead of me on Szechuen Road in front of the Episcopal church, a string of men; each had a Chinese lantern swinging in the air over his head, and they were singing and shouting as they zigzagged along the road, evidently having a jolly, good time, while Chinese on both sides of the road were seen dodging and scampering about in great fright in all directions, and acting as though they were chased by the Old Nick himself. I was at a distance of about one hundred yards from the scene. I took in the situation at once. My servant, who held a lantern ahead of me, to light the way, was so frightened that he began to come back towards me. I told him not to be afraid, but walk right straight ahead. Pretty soon we confronted three or four of the fellows, half tipsy. One of them snatched the lantern from my servant and another, staggering about, tried to give me a kick. I walked along coolly and unconcerned till I reached the last batch of two or three fellows. I found these quite sober and in their senses and they were lingering behind evidently to enjoy the fun and watch the crowd in their hilarious antics. I stopped and parleyed with them, and told them who I was. I asked them for the names of the fellows who snatched my boy's lantern and of the fellow who tried to kick me. They declined at first, but finally with the promise that I would not give them any trouble, they gave me the name of one of the fellows, his position on the vessel, and the name of the vessel he belonged to. It turned out that the man was the first mate of the ship "Eureka," the very vessel that brought me out to China, in 1855, and which happened to be consigned to the firm I was working for. The next morning, I wrote a note to the captain, asking him to hand the note to his first officer. The captain, on receiving the note, was quite excited, and handed it to the first mate, who immediately came ashore and apologized. I made it very pleasant for him and told him that Americans in China were held in high esteem by the people, and every American landing in China should be jealous of the high estimation in which they were held and not do anything to compromise it. My motive in writing the note was merely to get him on shore and give him this advice. He was evidently pleased with my friendly attitude and extended his hand for a shake to thank me for the advice. He invited me to go on board with him to take a glass of wine and be good friends. I thanked him for his offer, but declined it, and we parted in an amicable way.

My second incident, which happened a couple of months after the first, did not have such a peaceful ending.

After the partnership of the firm, in whose employ I was, dissolved, an auction sale of the furniture of the firm took place. In the room where the auction was proceeding, I happened to be standing in a mixed crowd of Chinese and foreigners. A stalwart six-footer of a Scotchman happened to be standing behind me. He was not altogether a stranger to me, for I had met him in the streets several times. He began to tie a bunch of cotton balls to my queue, simply for a lark. But I caught him at it and in a pleasant way held it up and asked him to untie it. He folded up his arms and drew himself straight up with a look of the utmost disdain and scorn. I at once took in the situation, and as my countenance sobered, I reiterated my demand to have the appendage taken off. All of a sudden, he thrust his fist against my mouth, without drawing any blood, however. Although he stood head and shoulders above me in height, yet I was not at all abashed or intimidated by his burly and contemptuous appearance. My dander was up and oblivious to all thoughts of our comparative size and strength, I struck him back in the identical place where he punched me, but my blow was a stinger and it went with lightning rapidity to the spot, without giving him time to think. It drew blood in great profusion from lip and nose. He caught me by the wrist with both his hands. As he held my right wrist in his powerful grasp, for he was an athlete and a sportsman, I was just on the point of raising my right foot for a kick, which was aimed at a vital point, when the head partner of the firm, who happened to be near, suddenly stepped in between and separated us. I then stood off to one side, facing my antagonist, who was moving off into the crowd. As I moved away, I was asked by a voice from the crowd:

"Do you want to fight?"

I said, "No, I was only defending myself. Your friend insulted me and added injury to insult. I took him for a gentleman, but he has proved himself a blackguard."

With this stinging remark, which was heard all over the room, I retired from the scene into an adjoining room, leaving the crowd to comment on the incident. The British Consul, who happened to be present on the occasion, made a casual remark on the merits of the case and said, as I was told afterwards by a friend, that "The young man was a little too fiery; if he had not taken the law into his own hands, he could have brought suit for assault and battery in the consular court, but since he has already retaliated and his last remark before the crowd has inflicted a deeper cut to his antagonist than the blow itself, he has lost the advantage of a suit."

The Scotchman, after the incident, did not appear in public for a whole week. I was told he had shut himself up in his room to give his wound time to heal, but the reason he did not care to show himself was more on account of being whipped by a little Chinaman in a public manner; for the affair, unpleasant and unfortunate as it was, created quite a sensation in the settlement. It was the chief topic of conversation for a short time among foreigners, while among the Chinese I was looked upon with great respect, for since the foreign settlement on the extra-territorial basis was established close to the city of Shanghai, no Chinese within its jurisdiction had ever been known to have the courage and pluck to defend his rights, point blank, when they had been violated or trampled upon by a foreigner. Their meek and mild disposition had allowed personal insults and affronts to pass unresented and unchallenged, which naturally had the tendency to encourage arrogance and insolence on the part of ignorant foreigners. The time will soon come, however, when the people of China will be so educated and enlightened as to know what their rights are, public and private, and to have the moral courage to assert and defend them whenever they are invaded. The triumph of Japan over Russia in the recent war has opened the eyes of the Chinese world. It will never tolerate injustice in any way or shape, much less will it put up with foreign aggression and aggrandizement any longer. They see now in what plight their national ignorance, conceit and conservatism, in which they had been fossilized, had placed them. They were on the verge of being partitioned by the European Powers and were saved from that catastrophe only by the timely intervention of the United States government. What the future will bring forth, since the Emperor Kwangsu and Dowager Empress Chi Hsi have both passed away, no one can predict.

The breaking up of the firm by which I was employed, once more, as stated before, and for the fourth time, threw me out of a regular business. But I was not at all disconcerted or discouraged, for I had no idea of following a mercantile life as a permanent calling. Within the past two years, my knowledge of the Chinese language had decidedly improved. I was not in hot haste to seek for a new position. I immediately took to translating as a means of bridging over the breaks of a desultory life. This independent avocation, though not a lucrative one, nevertheless led the way to a wider acquaintance with the educated and mercantile classes of the Chinese; to widen my acquaintance was my chief concern. My translating business brought me in contact with the comprador of one of the leading houses in Shanghai. The senior partner of this house died in 1857. He was well-known and thought much of by both the Chinese and the foreign mercantile body. To attest their high regard for his memory, the prominent Chinese merchants drew up an elaborate and eulogistic epitaph on the occasion of his death. The surviving members of the firm selected two translators to translate the epitaph. One was the interpreter in the British Consulate General, a brother to the author of "The Chinese and their Rebellions," and the other was (through the influence of the comprador) myself. To my great surprise, my translation was given the preference and accepted by the manager of the firm. The Chinese committee were quite elated that one of their countrymen knew enough English to bring out the inner sense of their epitaph. It was adopted and engraved on the monument. My name began to be known among the Chinese, not as a fighter this time, but as a Chinese student educated in America.

Soon after this performance, another event unexpectedly came up in which I was again called upon to act; that was the inundation of the Yellow River, which had converted the northern part of Kiangsu province into a sea, and made homeless and destitute thousands of people of that locality. A large body of refugees had wandered to and flocked near Shanghai. A Chinese deputation, consisting of the leading merchants and gentry, who knew or had heard of me, called and asked me to draw up a circular appealing to the foreign community for aid and contributions to relieve the widespread suffering among the refugees. Several copies were immediately put into circulation and in less than a week, no less than $20,000 were subscribed and paid. The Chinese Committee were greatly elated over their success and their joy was unbounded. To give a finishing touch to this stroke of business, I wrote in the name of the committee a letter of acknowledgment and thanks to the foreign community for the prompt and generous contribution it had made. This was published in the Shanghai local papers—"The Shanghai Mail" and "Friend of China"—so that inside of three months after I had started my translating business, I had become widely known among the Chinese as the Chinese student educated in America. I was indebted to Tsang Kee Foo, the comprador, for being in this line of business, and for the fact that I was becoming known in Shanghai. He was a well-educated Chinese—a man highly respected and trusted for his probity and intelligence. His long connection with the firm and his literary taste had gathered around him some of the finest Chinese scholars from all parts of China, while his business transactions brought him in touch with the leading Chinese capitalists and business men in Shanghai and elsewhere. It was through him that both the epitaph and the circular mentioned above were written; and it was Tsang Kee Foo who introduced me to the celebrated Chinese mathematician, Li Jen Shu, who years afterwards brought me to the notice of Viceroy Tsang Kwoh Fan—the distinguished general and statesman, who, as will be seen hereafter, took up and promoted the Chinese Education Scheme. In the great web of human affairs, it is almost impossible to know who among our friends and acquaintances may prove to be the right clue to unravel the skein of our destiny. Tsang Kee Foo introduced me to Li Jen Shu, the latter introduced me to Tsang Kwoh Fan, who finally through the Chinese Education Scheme grafted Western education to the Oriental culture, a union destined to weld together the different races of the world into one brotherhood.

My friend Tsang Kee Foo afterwards introduced me to the head or manager of Messrs. Dent & Co., who kindly offered me a position in his firm as comprador in Nagasaki, Japan, soon after that country was opened to foreign trade. I declined the situation, frankly and plainly stating my reason, which was that the compradorship, though lucrative, is associated with all that is menial, and that as a graduate of Yale, one of the leading colleges in America, I could not think of bringing discredit to my Alma Mater, for which I entertained the most profound respect and reverence, and was jealous of her proud fame. What would the college and my class-mates think of me, if they should hear that I was a comprador—the head servant of servants in an English establishment? I said there were cases when a man from stress of circumstances may be compelled to play the part of a menial for a shift, but I was not yet reduced to that strait, though I was poor financially. I told him I would prefer to travel for the firm as its agent in the interior and correspond directly with the head of the firm. In that case, I would not sacrifice my manhood for the sake of making money in a position which is commonly held to be servile. I would much prefer to pack tea and buy silk as an agent—either on a salary or on commission. Such was my ground for declining. I, however, thanked him for the offer. This interview took place in the presence of my friend, Tsang Kee Foo, who without knowing the details of the conversation, knew enough of the English language to follow the general tenor of the talk. I then retired and left the manager and my friend to talk over the result. Tsang afterwards told me that Webb said, "Yung Wing is poor but proud. Poverty and pride usually go together, hand in hand." A few days afterwards Tsang informed me that Webb had decided to send me to the tea districts to see and learn the business of packing tea.

IX

My First Trip to the Tea Districts

O n the 11th of March, 1859, I found myself on board of a Woo-Sik-Kwei, a Chinese boat built in Woo-Sik, a city situated on the borders of the Grand Canal, within a short distance of the famous city of Suchau—a rival of the city of Hangchau, for wealth, population, silk manufacture, and luxury. The word "Kwei" means "fast." Therefore, Woo-Sik-Kwei means fast boats of Woo-Sik. These passenger boats which plied between the principal cities and marts situated near the waters of the canal and lake system in southern Kianksu, were usually built of various sizes and nicely fitted up for the comfort and convenience of the public. Those intended for officials, and the wealthy classes, were built on a larger scale and fitted up in a more pretentious style. They were all flat-bottom boats. They sailed fairly well before the wind, but against it, they were either tracked by lines from the mast to the trackers on shore, or by sculling, at which the Chinese are adepts. They can give a boat a great speed by a pair of sculls resting on steel pivots that are fastened at the stern, one on each side, about the middle of the scull, with four men on each scull; the blades are made to play in the water astern, right and left, which pushes and sends the boat forward at a surprisingly rapid rate. But in recent years, steam has made its way into China and steam launches have superseded these native craft which are fast disappearing from the smooth waters of Kiangsu province—very much as the fast sailing ships, known as Baltimore Clippers, that in the fifties and sixties were engaged in the East India and China trade, have been gradually swept from the ocean by steam.

At the end of three days, I was landed in the historic city of Hangchau, which is the capital of Chêhkiang. It is situated on a plain of uneven ground, with hills in the southwest and west, and northeast. It covers an area of about three or four square miles. It is of a rectangular shape. Its length is from north to south; its breadth, from east to west. On the west, lies the Si-Hoo or West Lake, a beautiful sheet of limpid water with a gravelly or sandy bottom, stretching from the foot of the city wall to the foot of the mountains which appear in the distance in the rear, rising into the clouds like lofty bulwarks guarding the city on the north.

The Tsientang River, about two miles distant, flanks the city on the east. It takes its rise from the high mountain range of Hwui Chow in the southeast and follows a somewhat irregular course to the bay of the same name, and rushes down the rocky declivities like a foaming steed and empties itself into the bay about forty miles east of the city. This is one of the rivers that have periodical bores in which the tidal waters in their entrance to the bay create a noise like thunder, and the waves rise to the height of eight or ten feet.

Hangchau, aside from her historic fame as having been the seat of the government of the Sung Dynasty of the 12th and 13th centuries, has always maintained a wide reputation for fine buildings, public and private, such as temples, pagodas, mosques and bridges, which go to lend enchantment to the magnificent natural scenery with which she is singularly endowed. But latterly, age and the degeneration of the times have done their work of mischief. Her past glory is fast sinking into obscurity; she will never recover her former prestige, unless a new power arises to make her once more the capital of a regenerated government.

On the 15th of March, I left Hangchau to ascend the Tsientang River, at a station called Kang Kow, or mouth of the river, about two miles east of the city, where boats were waiting for us. Several hundreds of these boats of a peculiar and unique type were riding near the estuary of the river. These boats are called Urh Woo, named after the district where they were built. They vary from fifty to one hundred feet in length, from stem to stern, and are ten or fifteen feet broad, and draw not more than two or three feet of water when fully loaded. They are all flat-bottom boats, built of the most limber and flexible material that can be found, as they are expected to meet strong currents and run against rocks, both in their ascent and descent, on account of the irregularity and rocky bottom of the river. These boats, when completely equipped and covered with bamboo matting, look like huge cylinders, and are shaped like cigars. The interior from stem to stern is divided into separate compartments, or rooms, in which bunks are built to accommodate passengers. These compartments and bunks are removed when room is needed for cargoes. These boats ply between Hangchau and Sheong Shan and do all the interior transportation by water between these entrepôts in Chêhkiang and Kiangsi. Sheong Shan is the important station of Chêhkiang, and Yuh-Shan is that of Kiangsi. The distance between the two entrepôts is about fifty lis, or about sixteen English miles, connected by one of the finest macadamized roads in China. The road is about thirty feet wide, paved with slabs of granite and flanked with greenish-colored cobbles. A fine stone arch which was erected as a land-mark of the boundary line separating Chêhkiang and Kiangsi provinces, spans the whole width of the road. On both sides of the key-stone of the arch are carved four fine Chinese characters, painted in bright blue, viz., Leang Hsing Tung Chu:

This is one of the most notable arch-ways through which the inter-provincial trade has been carried on for ages past. At the time when I crossed from Sheong Shan to Yuh-Shan, the river ports of Hankau, Kiukiang, Wuhu and Chinkiang were not opened to foreign trade and steam-boats had not come in to play their part in the carrying trade of the interior of China. This magnificent thoroughfare was crowded with thousands of porters bearing merchandise of all kinds to and fro— exports and imports for distribution. It certainly presented an interesting sight to the traveller, as well as a profound topic of contemplation to a Chinese patriot.

The opening of the Yangtze River, which is navigable as far as Kingchau, on the borders of Szechwan province, commanding the trade of at least six or seven provinces along its whole course of nearly three thousand miles to the ocean, presents a spectacle of unbounded possibilities for the amelioration of nearly a third of the human race, if only the grasping ambition of the West will let the territorial integrity and the independent sovereignty of China remain intact. Give the people of China a fair chance to work out the problems of their own salvation, as for instance the solution of the labor question, which has been so radically disorganized and broken up by steam, electricity and machinery. This has virtually taken the breath and bread away from nine-tenths of the people of China, and therefore this immovable mass of population should be given ample time to recover from its demoralization.

To go back to my starting point at Kang Kow, the entrance to the river, two miles east of Hangchau, we set sail, with a fair wind, at five o'clock in the morning of the 15th of March, and in the evening at ten o'clock we anchored at a place named the "Seven Dragons," after having made about one hundred miles during the day. The eastern shore in this part of the Tsientang River is evidently of red sandstone formation, for we could see part of the strata submerged in the water, and excavations of the stone may be seen strewn about on the shore.

In fact, red sandstone buildings may be seen scattered about here and there. But the mountain about the Seven Dragons is picturesque and romantic.

Early the next day, we again started, but the rain poured down in torrents. We kept on till we reached the town of Lan Chi and came to anchor in the evening, after having made about forty miles. This is the favorite entrepôt where the Hupeh and Hunan congou teas were brought all the way from the tea districts of these provinces, to be housed and transhipped to Shanghai via Hangchau. Lan Chi is an entrepôt of only one street, but its entire length is six miles. It is famous for its nice hams, which are known all over China. On account of the incessant rain, we stopped half a day at Lan Chi. In the afternoon the sky began to clear and at twelve o'clock in the night we again started and reached the walled city of Ku Chow, which was besieged by the Taiping rebels in March, 1858, just a year before; after four months' duration the siege was raised and no great damage was done. We put up in an inn for the night. Ku Chow is a departmental city of Chêhkiang and is about thirty miles distant from Sheong Shan, already mentioned in connection with Yuh-Shan. We were delayed by the Custom House officials, as well as on account of the scarcity of porters and chair-bearers to take us over to Sheong Shan. We arrived at Yuh-Shan from Sheong Shan by chair in the evening. We put up in an inn for the night, having first engaged fishing boats to take us to the city of Kwangshun, thirty miles from Yuh-Shan, the next morning. After reaching Yuh-Shan, we were in Kiangsi territory, and our route now lay in a west by north direction, down stream towards the Po Yang Lake, whose southern margin we passed, and reached Nan Cheong, the capital of Kiangsi province. The city presented a fine outward appearance. We did not stop long enough to go through the city and see its actual condition since its evacuation by the rebels.

Our route from Nan Cheong was changed in a west by south direction, making the great entrepôt of Siang Tan our final goal. In this route, we passed quite a number of large cities that had nothing of special importance, either commercially or historically, to relate. We passed Cheong Sha, the capital of Hunan, in the night. We arrived at Siang Tan on the morning of the 15th of April. Siang Tan is one of the noted entrepôts in the interior of China and used to be the great distributing center of imports when foreign trade was confined to the single port of Canton. It was also the emporium where the tea and silk goods of China were centered and housed, to be carried down to Canton for exportation to foreign countries. The overland transport trade between Siang Tan and Canton was immense. It gave employment to at least one hundred thousand porters, carrying merchandise over the Nan Fung pass, between the two cities, and supported a large population along both sides of the thoroughfare. Steam, wars and treaties of very recent dates have not only broken up this system of labor and changed the complexion of the whole labor question throughout China, but will also alter the economical, industrial and political conditions of the Chinese Empire during the coming years of her history.

At Siang Tan, our whole party, composed of tea-men, was broken up and each batch began its journey to the district assigned it, to begin the work of purchasing raw tea and preparing it to be packed for shipment in Shanghai.

I stayed in Siang Tan about ten days and then made preparations for a trip up to the department of Kingchau in Hupeh province, to look into the yellow silk produced in a district called Ho-Yung.

We left Siang Tan on the 26th of April, and proceeded northward to our place of destination. Next morning at eight o'clock we reached Cheong Sha, the capital of Hunan province. As the day was wet and gloomy, we stopped and tried to make the best of it by going inside of the city to see whether there was anything worth seeing, but like all Chinese cities, it presented the same monotonous appearance of age and filth, the same unchangeable style of architecture and narrow streets. Early next morning, we resumed our boat journey, crossed the Tung Ting Lake and the great river Yangtze till we entered the mouth of the King Ho which carried us to Ho Yung. On this trip to hunt after the yellow silk—not the golden fleece—we were thirteen days from Siang Tan. The country on both banks of the King Ho seemed quiet and peaceful and people were engaged in agricultural pursuits. We saw many buffaloes and donkeys, and large patches of wheat, interspersed with beans. A novel sight presented itself which I have never met with elsewhere in China. A couple of country lassies were riding on a donkey, and were evidently in a happy mood, laughing and talking as they rode by. Arriving in Ho Yung, we had some difficulty in finding an inn, but finally succeeded in securing quarters in a silk hong. No sooner were we safely quartered, than a couple of native constables called to know who we were; our names and business were taken down. Our host, the proprietor of the hong, who knew the reason of our coming, explained things to the satisfaction of the men, who went away perfectly satisfied that we were honest traders and no rebel spies. We were left to transact our business unmolested. As soon as our object was known, numerous samples of yellow silk were brought for our inspection. We selected quite a number of samples, which altogether weighed about sixty-five pounds, and had them packed to be taken to Shanghai.

At the end of a fortnight, we concluded to take our journey back. Accordingly, on the 26th of May we bade Ho Yung farewell, and started for the tea district of Nih Kia Shi, in the department of Cheong Sha, via Hankau. We arrived at Hankau on the 5th of June, and put up in a native inn. The weather was hot and muggy, and our quarters were narrow and cut off from fresh air. Three days after our arrival, three deputies visited us to find out who we were. It did not take long to convince them that we were not rebel spies. We showed them the package of yellow silk, which bore marks of a war-tax which we had to pay on it, all along the route from Ho Yung to Hankau. We were left unmolested.

The port of Hankau had not been opened for foreign trade, though it was well understood that it was to be opened very soon. Before its capture by the Taiping rebels, or rather before the Taiping rebels had made their appearance on the stage of action, Hankau was the most important entrepôt in China. When the Taiping rebels captured Woochang in 1856, Hankau and Han Yang fell at the same time, and the port was destroyed by fire and was reduced to ashes. At the time of my visit, the whole place was rebuilt and trade began to revive. But the buildings were temporary shifts. Now the character of the place is completely changed and the foreign residences and warehouses along the water's edge have given it altogether a European aspect, so that the Hankau of today may be regarded as the Chicago or St. Louis of China, and in no distant day she is destined to surpass both in trade, population and wealth. I was in Hankau a few days before I crossed the Yangtze-Kiang to the black tea district of Nih Kia Shi.

We left Hankau on the 30th of June and went over to the tea packing houses in Nih Kia Shi and Yang Liu Tung on the 4th of July. I was in those two places over a month and gained a complete knowledge of the whole process of preparing the black tea for the foreign market. The process is very simple and can be easily learned. I do not know through what preparations the Indian and Assam teas have to go, where machinery is used, but they cannot be very elaborate. Undoubtedly, since the fifties, manual labor, the old standby in preparing teas for foreign consumption, has been much improved with a view of retaining a large percentage of the tea trade in China. The reason why a large percentage of the tea business has passed away from China to India is not because machinery is used in the one case and manual labor is retained in the other, but chiefly on account of the quality of the tea that is raised in the different soil of the two countries. The Indian or Assam tea is much stronger (in proportion to the same quantity) than the Chinese tea. The Indian tea is 2-1 to Chinese tea, in point of strength, whereas the Chinese tea is 2-1 to the Indian tea in point of delicacy and flavor. The Indian is rank and strong, but the Chinese tea is superior in the quality of its fine aroma. The higher class of tea-drinkers in America, Europe and Russia prefer China tea to Indian, whereas the laboring and common class in those countries take to Indian and Assam, from the fact that they are stronger and cheaper.

In the latter part of August I decided to return to Shanghai, not by way of Siang Tan, but via Hankau, down the Yangtze River to Kiu Kang and across the Poh Yang Lake. I arrived at Hankau again the second time on the 29th of August, having left there two months previous, in July. This time I came in a Hunan junk loaded with tea for Shanghai. At Ho Kow, the southern shore of the Poh Yang Lake, I had to follow the same route I took in March, and on the 21st of September I landed at Hangchau and from there I took a Woo-Sik-Kwei for Shanghai, where I arrived in the night of the 30th of September, the time consumed on this journey having been seven months—from March to October. It was my first journey into the interior of China, and it gave me a chance to gain an insight into the actual condition of the people, while a drastic rebellion was going on in their midst. The zone of the country through which I had passed had been visited by the rebels and the imperialists, but was, to all outward appearance, peaceful and quiet. To what extent the people had suffered both from rebel and imperialist devastations in those sections of the country, no one can tell. But there was one significant fact that struck me forcibly and that was the sparseness of population, which was at variance with my preconceived notions regarding the density of population in China which I had gathered from books and accounts of travelers. This was particularly noticeable through that section of Chêhkiang, Kiangsi, Hunan and Hupeh, which I visited. The time of the year, when crops of all kinds needed to be planted, should have brought out the peasantry into the open fields with oxen, mules, donkeys, buffaloes and horses, as indispensable accessories to farm life. But comparatively few farmers were met with.

Shortly after my arrival from the interior, in October, an English friend of mine requested me to go to Shau Hing to buy raw silk for him. Shau Hing is a city located in a silk district about twenty miles southwest of Hangchau, and noted for its fine quality of silk. I was about two months in this business, when I was taken down with fever and ague and was compelled to give it up. Shau Hing, like most Chinese cities, was filthy and unhealthy and the water that flowed through it was as black as ink. The city was built in the lowest depression of a valley, and the outlet of the river was so blocked that there was hardly any current to carry off the filth that had been accumulating for ages. Hence the city was literally located in a cesspool—a breeding place for fever and ague, and epidemics of all kinds. But I soon recovered from the attack of the fever and ague and as soon as I could stand on my legs again, I immediately left the malarial atmosphere, and was, in a short time, breathing fresher and purer air.

X

My Visit to the Taipings

In the fall of 1859 a small party of two missionaries, accompanied by Tsang Laisun, planned a trip to visit the Taiping rebels in Nanking. I was asked to join them, and I decided to do so. My object in going was to find out for my own satisfaction the character of the Taipings; whether or not they were the men fitted to set up a new government in the place of the Manchu Dynasty. Accordingly, on the 6th of November, 1859, we left Shanghai in a Woo-Sik-Kwei boat, with a stiff northeast breeze in our favor, though we had to stem an ebb tide for an hour. The weather was fine and the whole party was in fine spirits. We happened to have an American flag on board, and on the spur of the moment, it was flung to the breeze, but on a sober second thought, we had it hauled down so as not to attract undue attention and have it become the means of thwarting the purpose of our journey. Instead of taking the Sung-Kiang route which was the highway to Suchau, we turned off into another one in order to avoid the possibility of being hauled up by the imperialists and sent back to Shanghai, as we were told that an imperial fleet of Chinese gun-boats was at anchor at Sung Kiang. We found the surrounding country within a radius of thirty miles of Shanghai to be very quiet and saw no signs of political disturbance. The farmers were busily engaged in gathering in their rice crops.

It might be well to mention here that during my sojourn in the interior, the Taiping rebels had captured the city of Suchau, and there was some apprehension on the part of foreigners in the settlement that they might swoop down to take possession of the city of Shanghai, as well as the foreign settlement. That was the reason the Sung Kiang River was picketed by Chinese gun-boats, and the foreign pickets were extended miles beyond the boundary line of the foreign concession.

We reached Suchau on the morning of the 9th of November without meeting with any difficulty or obstacles all the way, nor were we challenged either by the imperialists or rebels, which went to show how loosely and negligently even in time of war, things were conducted in China. On arriving at the Lau Gate of the city, we had to wait at the station where tickets were issued to those who went into the city and taken from those who left, for Suchau was then under martial law. As we wished to go into the city to see the commandant, in order to get letters of introduction from him to the chiefs of other cities along our route to Nanking, we had to send two of our party to headquarters to find out whether we were permitted to enter. At the station, close to the Lau Gate, we waited over an hour. Finally our party appeared accompanied by the same messenger who had been deputed by the head of the police to accompany them to the commandant's office. Permission was given us, and all four went in. The civil officer was absent, but we were introduced to the military commandant, Liu. He was a tall man, dressed in red. His affected hauteur at the start was too thin to disguise his want of a solid character. He became very inquisitive and asked the object of our journey to Nanking. He treated us very kindly, however, and gave us a letter of introduction to the commandant in Tan Yang, and furnished us with passports all the way through the cities of Woo Sik and Cheong Chow. In the audience hall of Commandant Liu, we were introduced to four foreigners—two Americans, one Englishman, and a French noble. One of the Americans said he was a doctor, the Englishman was supposed to be a military officer, and the Frenchman, as stated above, claimed to be a nobleman. Doubtless they were all adventurers. Each had his own ax to grind. One of the Americans had a rifle and cartridges for sale. He asked quite an exorbitant price for them and they were summarily rejected. The Frenchman said he had lost a fortune and had come out to China to make it up. Our missionary companions were much pleased after being entertained by Liu in hearing him recite the doxology, which he did glibly. Towards evening, when we returned to our boat, he sent us a number of chickens and a goat to boot. We were thus amply provisioned to prosecute our journey to Tan Yang. We left Suchau on the morning of the 11th of November. On our arrival at Woo Sik, our passports were examined and we were very courteously treated by the rebels. We were invited to dinner by the chief in command. After that he sent us fruits and nuts, and came on board himself to see us off. We held quite a long conversation with him, which ended in his repeating the doxology.

November 12th we left Woo Sik and started for Cheong Chow. From Suchau onward we were on the Grand Canal. The road on the bank of the canal was in good condition. Most of the people we saw and met were rebels, traveling between Tan Yang and Suchau, and but few boats were seen passing each other. All the country surrounding the canal between those cities seemed to have been abandoned by the peasantry and the cultivated fields were covered with rank grass and weeds, instead of flourishing crops. A traveler, not knowing the circumstances, would naturally lay the blame wholly upon the Taiping rebels, but the imperialists in their conflicts with the rebels, were as culpable as their enemies. The rebels whom we met on the public road were generally very civil and tried in every way to protect the people in order to gain their confidence. Incendiarism, pillage, robbery and ill-treatment of the people by the rebels, were punished by death. We reached Cheong Chow in the night. We found nearly all the houses along the road between Woo Sik and Cheong Chow to be completely deserted and emptied of all their inmates. There were occasionally a few of the inhabitants to be seen standing on the bank with small baskets, peddling eggs, oranges and cakes, vegetables and pork. They were principally old people, with countenances showing their suffering and despair. On November 13, at six o'clock in the morning, we resumed our journey to Tan Yang. As we drew near Tan Yang, the people seemed to have regained their confidence and the fields seemed to be cultivated. The conduct of the rebels towards them was considerate and commendable. During the morning we saw a force of one thousand men marching towards Tan Yang. We did not quite reach Tan Yang and came to anchor for the night in plain sight of it.

Early next morning, we went into the city to see the Commandant Liu, to present to him the letter we received in Suchau, but he was absent from the city. The man next to Liu, a civilian, came out to meet us. He was very affable and treated us kindly and with great civility. One of our party referred to the religious character of the Taipings.

Chin then gave us his views of Christianity, as taught by Hung Siu Chune—the leader of the rebellion. He said:

"We worship God the Heavenly Father, with whom Jesus and the Holy Spirit constitute the true God; that Shang Ti is the True Spirit."

He then repeated the doxology. He said the rebels had two doxologies—the old and the new; they had discarded the new and adopted the old. He said, the Tien Wong—the Celestial Emperor—was taken up to Heaven and received orders from the Heavenly Father to come and exterminate all evil and rectify all wrong; to destroy idolatry and evil spirits, and finally to teach the people the knowledge of God. He did not know whether the Tien Wong was translated to Heaven bodily or in spirit, or both. He said the Tien Wong himself explained that he could not hold the same footing with God himself; that the homage paid to God was an act of religious worship, but that rendered to the Tien Wong was merely an act of court etiquette, which ministers and officers always paid to their sovereigns in every dynasty, and could not be construed as acts of worship. He also said that Tien Wong was a younger brother of Christ, but that it did not follow that he was born of the same mother. Tien Wong, he claimed, was a younger brother of Christ in the sense that he was especially appointed by God to instruct the people. Christ was also appointed by God to reform and redeem the world. With regard to the three cups of tea,—he said that they were intended as a thank-offering, and were not propitiatory in their character.

"Whenever we drink a cup of tea, we offer thanksgiving to the Heavenly Father. The three cups of tea have no reference to the Trinity whatever. One cup answers the same purpose. The number three was purposely chosen, because it is the favorite number with the Chinese,—it is even mentioned in the Chinese classics."

As for redemption, he said,—"No sacrificial offering can take away our sins; the power of redemption is in Christ; he redeems us and it is our duty to repent of our sins. Even the Tien Wong is very circumspect and is afraid to sin against God."

In the matter of the soldiery keeping aloof from the people in time of war, he said,—"It has been an immemorial custom, adopted by almost every dynasty, that the people should go to the country, and the soldiers be quartered in the city. When a city is captured or taken, it is easy to subjugate the surrounding country."

The places we saw in ruins, both at Suchau and all the way up the canal, were partly destroyed by Cheong Yuh Leang's troops in their retreat, partly by local predatory parties for the sake of plunder, and partly by the Taipings themselves. When Chung Wong was in Suchau, he did all he could to suppress incendiarism by offering rewards of both money and rank to those who took an active part in suppressing it. He issued three orders: 1. That soldiers were not allowed to kill or slaughter the inhabitants. 2. They were prohibited from slaughtering cattle. 3. They were prohibited from setting fire to houses. A violation of any of these orders was attended with capital punishment. When he came down to Woo Sik, he had a country elder decapitated for allowing local bandits to burn down the houses of the people. This was the information we gathered from our conversation with Chin. He also said that Ying Wong and Chung Wong were both talented men—not only in military but also in civil affairs.

He gave us a long account of the capture of different places by the rebels, and how they had been defeated before Nanking, when that city was laid siege to by the imperialists in the early part of 1860. He also showed us a letter by a chief at Hwui Chow regarding the utter defeat and rout of Tsang Kwoh Fan, who was hemmed in by an immense force of the rebels. Tsang was supposed to have been killed in the great battle. He said that Cheong Yuh Leang, the imperialist general, who laid siege to Nanking, after his defeat went to Hangchau for medical treatment for hemorrhage of the lungs; that all the country along the canal, north of the Yangtze, was in the hands of the rebels, and that Princes Chung and Ying were marching up the river to take possession of Hupeh, and that Shih Ta Kai, another chief, was assigned the conquest of Yun Nan, Kwai Chow and Sze Chune provinces. At that time Chin Kiang was being besieged by the rebels, and Chi Wong was in command of an army of observation in Kiang Nan. Such was the rambling statement given us by Chin regarding the disposition of the rebel forces under different chiefs or princes.

After dining with him in the evening, we repaired to our boat for the night. The next morning, November 15th, we again went into the city and called upon Liu, but, failing to see him, we again called upon Chin to arrange for the conveyance of our luggage and ourselves from Tan Yang to Nanking. The aide told us to send all our things to Chin's office and that our boat, if left in Tan Yang until our return, would be well cared for and protected during our absence. So next morning, the 16th of November, we started on foot and walked fifteen miles from Tan Yang to a village called Po Ying, about six miles from the city of Ku Yung, where we halted to pass the night. We had some difficulty in securing a resting place. The people were poor and had no confidence in strangers. We, however, after some coaxing, were supplied with straws spread out on the ground, and the next morning we gave the old women a dollar. We had boiled rice gruel, cold chicken and crackers for our breakfast. When we reached Ku Yung about nine o'clock on the 17th of November, we found that every gate of the city was closed against us, as well as all others, because a rumor was afloat that the rebels before Chin Kiang were defeated, and that they were flocking towards Ku Yung for shelter. So we concluded to continue on our journey towards Nanking, though our missionary friends came near deciding to return to Tan Yang and wend our way back to Shanghai. We proceeded not far from Ku Yung, when we finally succeeded in getting chairs and mules to prosecute our journey.

On the 18th of November, after a trying and wearisome journey, we reached Nanking. I was the first one to reach the South Gate, waiting for the rest of the party to come up before entering. We were reported inside of the gate and messengers accompanied us to the headquarters of the Rev. Mr. Roberts, close by the headquarters of Hung Jin, styled Prince Kan.

After our preliminary introduction to the Rev. Mr. Roberts, I excused myself, and leaving the rest of the party to continue their conversation with him, retired to my quarters to clean up and get rested from the long and tedious journey. In fact, I had little or nothing to say while in Mr. Roberts' presence, nor did I attempt to make myself known to him. I had seen him often in Macao when in Mrs. Gutzlaff's school, twenty or more years before, and I had recognized him at once as soon as I set my eyes on him. He certainly appeared old to me, being dressed in his yellow satin robe of state and moving leisurely in his clumsy Chinese shoes. Exactly in what capacity he was acting in Nanking, I was at a loss to know; whether still as a religious adviser to Hung Siu Chune, or playing the part of secretary of state for the Taiping Dynasty, no one seemed able to tell.

The next day (the 19th of November) I was invited to call on Kan Wong. He was a nephew of Hung Siu Chune, the rebel chief who was styled Tien Wong or the Celestial Sovereign. Before Hung Jin came to Nanking, I had made his acquaintance, in 1856, at Hong Kong. He was then connected with the London Mission Association as a native preacher and was under Dr. James Legge, the distinguished translator of the Chinese classics. I saw considerable of him while in Hong Kong and even then he had expressed a wish that he might see me some day in Nanking. He was then called Hung Jin, but since he had joined his uncle in Nanking, he was raised to the position of a prince. Kan means "Protecting," and Kan Wong signifies "Protecting Prince." He greeted me very cordially and evidently was glad to see me. After the usual exchange of conventionalities, he wanted to know what I thought of the Taipings; whether I thought well enough of their cause to identify myself with it. In reply, I said I had no intention of casting my lot with them, but came simply to see him and pay my respects. At the same time, I wanted to find out for my own satisfaction the actual condition of things in Nanking. I said the journey from

Suchau to Nanking had suggested several things to me, which I thought might be of interest to him. They were as follows:

1. To organize an army on scientific principles.
2. To establish a military school for the training of competent military officers.
3. To establish a naval school for a navy.
4. To organize a civil government with able and experienced men to act as advisers in the different departments of administration.
5. To establish a banking system, and to determine on a standard of weight and measure.
6. To establish an educational system of graded schools for the people, making the Bible one of the text books.
7. To organize a system of industrial schools.

These were the topics that suggested themselves to me during the journey. If the Taiping government would be willing, I said, to adopt these measures and set to work to make suitable appropriations for them, I would be perfectly willing to offer my services to help carry them out. It was in that capacity that I felt I could be of the most service to the Taiping cause. In any other, I would simply be an encumbrance and a hindrance to them.

Such was the outcome of my first interview. Two days later, I was again invited to call. In the second interview, we discussed the merits and the importance of the seven proposals stated in our first interview. Kan Wong, who had seen more of the outside world than the other princes or leaders, and even more than Hung Siu Chune himself, knew wherein lay the secret of the strength and power of the British government and other European powers, and fully appreciated the paramount importance and bearing of these proposals. But he was alone and had no one to back him in advocating them. The other princes, or leaders, were absent from the city, carrying on their campaign against the imperialists. He said he was well aware of the importance of these measures, but nothing could be done until they returned, as it required the consent of the majority to any measure before it could be carried out.

A few days after this a small parcel was presented to me as coming from Kan Wong. On opening it, I found to my great surprise a wooden seal about four inches long and an inch wide, having my name carved with the title of "E," which means "Righteousness," and designates the fourth official rank under that of a prince, which is the first. My title was written out on a piece of yellow satin stamped with the official seal of the Kan Wong. I was placed in a quandary and was at a loss to know its purport,—whether it was intended to detain me in Nanking for good or to commit me irretrievably to the Taiping cause, *nolens volens*. At all events, I had not been consulted in the matter and Kan Wong had evidently acted on his own responsibility and taken it for granted that by conferring on me such a high rank as the fourth in the official scale of the Taipings, I might be induced to accept and thus identify myself with the Taiping cause—of the final success of which I had strong doubts, judging from the conduct, character and policy of the leading men connected with it. I talked the matter over with my associates, and came to the decision that I must forthwith return the seal and decline the tempting bauble. I went in person to thank Kan Wong for this distinguished mark of his high consideration, and told him that at any time when the leaders of the Taipings decided to carry out either one or all of my suggestions, made in my first interview with him, I should be most happy to serve them, if my services were needed to help in the matter. I then asked him as a special favor for a passport that would guarantee me a safe conduct in traveling through the territory under the jurisdiction of the Taipings, whether on business or pleasure. The passport was issued to me the next day, on the 24th of December, and we were furnished with proper conveyances and provisions to take us back to the city of Tan Yang, where our boat lay under the protection of Chin, second in command of the city, waiting our return from Nanking. We started on our return trip for Shanghai on the 27th of December by the same route as we came, and arrived safely in Tan Yang in the early part of January, 1861.

On my way back to Shanghai, I had ample time to form an estimate of the Taiping Rebellion—its origin, character and significance.

XI

REFLECTIONS ON THE TAIPING REBELLION

Rebellions and revolutions in China are not new and rare historic occurrences. There have been at least twenty-four dynasties and as many attendant rebellions or revolutions. But with the exception of the Feudatory period, revolutions in China (since the consolidation of the three Kingdoms into one Empire under the Emperor Chin) meant only a change of hands in the government, without a change either of its form, or principles. Hence the history of China for at least two thousand years, like her civilization, bears the national impress of a monotonous dead level—jejune in character, wanting in versatility of genius, and almost devoid of historic inspiration.

The Taiping Rebellion differs from its predecessors in that in its embryo stage it had taken onto itself the religious element, which became the vital force that carried it from the defiles and wilds of Kwangsi province in the southwest to the city of Nanking in the northeast, and made it for a period of fifteen years a constantly impending danger to the Manchu Dynasty, whose corruption, weakness and maladministration were the main causes that evoked the existence of this great rebellion.

The religious element that gave it life and character was a foreign product, introduced into China by the early Protestant missionaries, of whom Dr. Robert Morrison was the first English pioneer sent out by the London Mission, followed a decade later by the Rev. Icabod J. Roberts, an American missionary. These two missionaries may properly claim the credit, if there is any, of having contributed (each in his particular sphere) in imparting to Hung Siu Chune a knowledge of Christianity. Dr. Morrison, on his part, had translated the Bible into Chinese, and the Emperor Khang Hsi's dictionary into English; both these achievements gave the missionary work in China a basis to go upon in prosecuting the work of revising and of bringing the Bible to the Chinese standard of literary taste, so as to commend it to the literary classes, and in making further improvements in perfecting the Chinese-English dictionary, which was subsequently done by such men as Dr. Medhurst, Bishop Boone, Dr. Legge, E. C. Bridgeman, and S. Wells Williams.

Besides these works of translation, which undoubtedly called for further revision and improvement, Dr. Morrison also gave China a native convert—Leang Ahfah—who became afterwards a noted preacher and the author of some religious tracts.

Hung Siu Chune, in his quest after religious knowledge and truths, got hold of a copy of Dr. Morrison's Bible and the tracts of Leang Ahfah. He read and studied them, but he stood in need of a teacher to explain to him many points in the Bible, which appeared to him mysterious and obscure. He finally made the acquaintance of the Rev. Mr. Icabod J. Roberts, an American missionary from Missouri, who happened to make his headquarters in Canton. Hung Siu Chune called upon him often, till their acquaintance ripened into a close and lasting friendship, which was kept up till Hung Siu Chune succeeded in taking Nanking, when Mr. Roberts was invited to reside there in the double capacity of a religious teacher and a state adviser. This was undoubtedly done in recognition of Mr. Roberts' services as Hung's teacher and friend while in Canton. No one knew what had become of Mr. Roberts when Nanking fell and reverted to the imperialists in 1864.

It was about this time, when he was sedulously seeking Mr. Roberts' religious instructions at Canton, that Hung failed to pass his first competitive examination as a candidate to compete for official appointment, and he decided to devote himself exclusively to the work of preaching the Gospel to his own people, the Hakkas of Kwang Tung and Kwangsi. But as a colporter and native preacher, Hung had not reached the climax of his religious experience before taking up his stand as the leader of his people in open rebellion against the Manchu Dynasty.

We must go back to the time when, as a candidate for the literary competitive examinations, he was disappointed. This threw him into a fever, and when he was tossing about in delirium, he was supposed to have been translated to Heaven, where he was commanded by the Almighty to fill and execute the divine mission of his life, which was to destroy idolatry, to rectify all wrong, to teach the people a knowledge of the true God, and to preach redemption through Christ. In view of such a mission, and being called to the presence of God, he at once assumed himself to be the son of God, co-equal with Christ, whom he called his elder brother.

It was in such a state of mental hallucination that Hung Siu Chune appeared before his little congregation of Hakkas—migrating strangers—in the defiles and wilds of Kwangsi. Their novel and strange conduct as worshippers of Shangti—the Supreme Ruler—their daily religious exercises, their prayers, and their chanting of the doxology as taught and enjoined by him, had attracted a widespread attention throughout all the surrounding region of Kwangsi. Every day fresh accessions of new comers flocked to their fold and swelled their ranks, till their numerical force grew so that the local mandarins were baffled and at their wits' end to know what to do with these believers of Christianity. Such, in brief, was the origin, growth and character of the Christian element working among the simple and rustic mountaineers of Kwangsi and Kwang Tung.

It is true that their knowledge of Christianity, as sifted through the medium of the early missionaries from the West, and the native converts and colporters, was at best crude and elementary, but still they were truths of great power, potential enough to turn simple men and religiously-inclined women into heroes and heroines who faced dangers and death with the utmost indifference, as was seen subsequently, when the government had decided to take the bull by the horns and resorted to persecution as the final means to break up this religious, fanatical community. In their conflicts with the imperial forces, they had neither guns nor ammunition, but fought with broomsticks, flails and pitchforks. With these rustic and farming implements they drove the imperialist hordes before them as chaff and stubble before a hurricane. Such was their pent-up religious enthusiasm and burning ardor.

Now this religious persecution was the side issue that had changed the resistance of Hung Siu Chune and his followers, in their religious capacity, into the character of a political rebellion. It is difficult to say whether or not, if persecution had not been resorted to, Hung Siu Chune and his followers would have remained peaceably in the heart of China and developed a religious community. We are inclined to think, however, that even if there had been no persecution, a rebellion would have taken place, from the very nature of the political situation.

Neither Christianity nor religious persecution was the immediate and logical cause of the rebellion of 1850. They might be taken as incidents or occasions that brought it about, but they were not the real causes of its existence. These may be found deeply seated in the vitals of the political constitution of the government. Foremost among them was the corruption of the administrative government. The whole official organization, from head to foot, was honeycombed and tainted by a system of bribery, which passed under the polite and generic term of "presents," similar in character to what is now known as "graft." Next comes the exploitation of the people by the officials, who found an inexhaustible field to build up their fortunes. Finally comes the inevitable and logical corollary to official bribery and exploitation, namely, that the whole administrative government was founded on a gigantic system of fraud and falsehood.

This rebellion rose in the arena of China with an enigmatic character like that of the Sphinx, somewhat puzzling at the start. The Christian world throughout the whole West, on learning of its Christian tendencies, such as the worship of the true and living God; Christ the Savior of the world; the Holy Spirit, the purifier of the soul; the destruction of temples and idols that was found wherever their victorious arms carried them; the uncompromising prohibition of the opium habit; the observance of a Sabbath; the offering of prayers before and after meals; the invocation of divine aid before a battle—all these cardinal points of a Christian faith created a world-wide impression that China, through the instrumentality of the Taipings, was to be evangelized; that the Manchu Dynasty was to be swept out of existence, and a "Celestial Empire of Universal Peace," as it was named by Hung Siu Chune, was going to be established, and thus China, by this wonderful intervention of a wise Providence, would be brought within the pale of Christian nations. But Christendom was a little too credulous and impulsive in the belief. It did not stop to have the Christianity of the Taipings pass through the crucible of a searching analysis.

Their first victory over their persecutors undoubtedly gave Hung Siu Chune and his associates the first intimation of a possible overturning of the Manchu Dynasty and the establishment of a new one, which he named in his religious ecstasy "The Celestial Empire of Universal Peace." To the accomplishment of this great object, they bent the full force of their iconoclastic enthusiasm and religious zeal.

En route from Kwang Si, their starting point, to Nanking, victory had perched on their standard all the way. They had despatched a division of their army to Peking, and, on its way to the northern capitol, it had met with a repulse and defeat at Tientsin from whence they had turned back to Nanking. In their victorious march through Hunan, Hupeh, Kiang Si and part of An Hwui, their depleted forces were replenished and reinforced by fresh and new accessions gathered from the people of those provinces. They were the riffraff and scum of their populations.

This rabble element added no new strength to their fighting force, but proved to be an encumbrance and caused decided weakness. They knew no discipline, and had no restraining religious power to keep them from pillage, plunder and indiscriminate destruction. It was through such new accessions that the Taiping cause lost its prestige, and was defeated before Tientsin and forced to retreat to Nanking. After their defeat in the North, they began to decline in their religious character and their bravery. Their degeneracy was accelerated by the capture of Yang Chow, Suchau, and Hangchau, cities noted in Chinese history for their great wealth as well as for their beautiful women. The capture of these centers of a materialistic civilization poured into their laps untold wealth and luxury which tended to hasten their downfall.

The Taiping Rebellion, after fifteen years of incessant and desultory fighting, collapsed and passed into oblivion, without leaving any traces of its career worthy of historical commemoration beyond the fact that it was the outburst of a religious fanaticism which held the Christian world in doubt and bewilderment, by reason of its Christian origin. It left no trace of its Christian element behind either in Nanking, where it sojourned for nearly ten years, or in Kwang Si, where it had its birth. In China, neither new political ideas nor political theories or principles were discovered which would have constituted the basal facts of a new form of government. So that neither in the religious nor yet in the political world was mankind in China or out of China benefited by that movement. The only good that resulted from the Taiping Rebellion was that God made use of it as a dynamic power to break up the stagnancy of a great nation and wake up its consciousness for a new national life, as subsequent events in 1894, 1895, 1898, 1900, 1901, and 1904–5 fully demonstrated.

XII

Expedition to the Taiping Tea District

My Nanking visit was utterly barren of any substantial hope of promoting any scheme of educational or political reform for the general welfare of China or for the advancement of my personal interest. When I was thoroughly convinced that neither the reformation nor the regeneration of China was to come from the Taipings, I at once turned my thoughts to the idea of making a big fortune as my first duty, and as the first element in the successful carrying out of other plans for the future.

One day, while sauntering about in the tea garden inside the city of Shanghai, I came across a few tea-merchants regaling themselves with that beverage in a booth by themselves, evidently having a very social time. They beckoned to me to join their party. In the course of the conversation, we happened to touch on my late journey through the tea districts of Hunan, Hupeh and Kiang Si and also my trip to Nanking. Passing from one topic of conversation to another, we lighted upon the subject of the green tea district of Taiping in An Hwui province. It was stated that an immense quantity of green tea could be found there, all packed and boxed ready for shipment, and that the rebels were in possession of the goods, and that whoever had the hardihood and courage to risk his life to gain possession of it would become a millionaire. I listened to the account with deep and absorbing interest, taking in everything that was said on the subject. It was stated that there were over 1,000,000 chests of tea there. Finally the party broke up, and I wended my way to my quarters completely absorbed in deep thought. I reasoned with myself that this was a chance for me to make a fortune, but wondered who would be foolhardy enough to furnish the capital, thinking that no business man of practical experience would risk his money in such a wild goose adventure, surrounded as it was with more than ordinary dangers and difficulties, in a country where highway robbery, lawlessness and murder were of daily occurrence. But with the glamor of a big fortune confronting me, all privations, dangers and risks of life seemed small and faded into airy nothing.

My friend, Tsang Mew, who had been instrumental in having me sent traveling into the interior a year before, was a man of great business experience. He had a long head and a large circle of business acquaintances, besides being my warm friend, so I concluded to go to him and talk over the whole matter, as I knew he would not hesitate to give me his best advice. I laid the whole subject before him. He said he would consider the matter fully and in a few days let me know what he had decided to do about it. After a few days, he told me that he had had several consultations with the head of the firm, of which he was comprador, and between them the company had decided to take up my project.

The plan of operation as mapped out by me was as follows: I was to go to the district of Taiping by the shortest and safest route possible, to find out whether the quantity of tea did exist; whether it was safe to have treasure taken up there to pay the rebels for the tea; and whether it was possible to have the tea supply taken down by native boats to be transhipped by steamer to Shanghai. This might be called the preliminary expedition. Then, I was to determine which of the two routes would be the more feasible,—there being two, one by way of Wuhu, a treaty port, and another by way of Ta Tung, not a treaty port, a hundred miles above Wuhu. Wuhu and the whole country leading to Taiping, including the district itself, was under the jurisdiction of the rebels, whereas Ta Tung was still in possession of the imperialists. From Wuhu to Taiping by river the distance was about two hundred and fifty miles, whereas, by way of Ta Tung, the way, though shorter, was mostly overland, which made transportation more difficult and expensive, besides having to pay the imperialists a heavy war-tax at Ta Tung, while duty and war-tax were entirely free at Wuhu.

In this expedition of inspection, I chose Wuhu as the basis of my operation. I started with four Chinese tea-men, natives of Taiping who had fled to Shanghai as refugees when the whole district was changed into a theatre of bloody conflicts between the imperialist and rebel forces for two years. On the way up the Wuhu River, we passed three cities mostly deserted by their inhabitants, but occupied by rebels. Paddy fields on both sides of the river were mostly left uncultivated and deserted, overrun with rank weeds and tall grass. As we ascended towards Taiping, the whole region presented a heartrending and depressing scene of wild waste and devastation. Whole villages were depopulated and left in a dilapidated condition. Out of a population of 500,000 only a few dozen people were seen wandering about in a listless, hopeless condition, very much emaciated and looking like walking skeletons.

After a week's journey we reached the village of San Kow, where we were met and welcomed by three tea-men who had been in Shanghai about four years previous. It seemed that they had succeeded in weathering the storm which had swept away the bulk of the population and left them among the surviving few. They were mighty glad to see us, and our appearance in the village seemed to be a God-send. Among the houses that were left intact, I selected the best of them to be my headquarters for the transaction of the tea business. The old tea-men were brought in to co-operate in the business and they showed us where the tea was stored. I was told that in San Kow there were at least five hundred thousand boxes, but in the whole district of Taiping there were at least a million and a half boxes, about sixty pounds of tea to a box.

At the end of another week, I returned to Wuhu and reported all particulars. I had found that the way up from Wuhu by river to Taiping was perfectly safe and I did not anticipate any danger to life or treasure. I had seen a large quantity of the green tea myself and found out that all that was needed was to ship as much treasure as it was safe to have housed in Wuhu, and from there to have it transferred in country tea-boats, well escorted by men in case of any emergency. I also sent samples of the different kinds of green tea to Shanghai to be inspected and listed. These proved to be satisfactory, and the order came back to buy as much of the stock as could be bought.

I was appointed the head of all succeeding expeditions to escort treasure up the river to San Kow and cargoes of tea from there to Wuhu. In one of these expeditions, I had a staff of six Europeans and an equal number of Chinese tea-men. We had eight boxes of treasure containing altogether Tls. 40,000. A tael, in the sixties, according to the exchange of that period, was equal to $1.33, making the total amount in Mexican dollars to be a little over $53,000. We had a fleet of eight tea-boats, four large ones and four smaller ones. The treasure was divided into two equal parts and was placed in the two largest and staunchest boats. The men were also divided into two squads, three Europeans and three Chinese in one large boat and an equal number in the other. We were well provided with firearms, revolvers and cutlasses. Besides the six Europeans, we had about forty men including the boatmen, but neither the six tea-men nor the boatmen could be relied upon to show fight in case of emergency. The only reliable men I had to fall back upon, in case of emergency, were the Europeans; even in these I was not sure I could place implicit confidence, for they were principally runaway sailors of an adventurous character picked up in Shanghai by the company and sent up to Wuhu to escort the treasure up to the interior. Among them was an Englishman who professed to be a veterinary doctor. He was over six feet tall in his stocking feet, a man of fine personal appearance, but he did not prove himself to be of very stout heart, as may be seen presently. Thus prepared and equipped, we left Wuhu in fine spirits. We proceeded on our journey a little beyond the city of King Yuen, which is about half the way to San Kow. We could have gone a little beyond King Yuen, but thinking it might be safer to be near the city, where the rebel chief had seen my passport, obtained in Nanking, and knew that I had influential people in Nanking, we concluded to pass the night in a safe secluded little cove in the bend of the river just large enough for our little boats to moor close to each other, taking due precaution to place the two largest ones in the center, flanked by the other boats on the right and left of them; the smaller boats occupied the extreme ends of the line.

Before retiring, I had ordered all our firearms to be examined and loaded and properly distributed. Watchmen were stationed in each boat to keep watch all night, for which they were to be paid extra. The precautionary steps having thus been taken, we all retired for the night. An old tea-man and myself were the only ones who lay wide awake while the rest gave unmistakable signs of deep sleep. I felt somewhat nervous and could not sleep. The new moon had peeked in upon us occasionally with her cold smile, as heavy and dark clouds were scudding across her path. Soon she was shut in and disappeared, and all was shrouded in pitch darkness. The night was nearly half spent, when my ears caught the distant sound of whooping and yelling which seemed to increase in volume. I immediately started up to dress myself and quietly woke up the Europeans and Chinese in both boats. As the yelling and whooping drew nearer and nearer it seemed to come from a thousand throats, filling the midnight air with unearthly sounds. In another instant countless torch lights were seen dancing and whirling in the dismal darkness right on the opposite bank. Fortunately the river was between this marauding band and us, while pitch darkness concealed our boats from their sight. In view of such impending danger, we held a council of war. None of us were disposed to fight and endanger our lives in a conflict in which the odds were fearfully against us, there being about a thousand to one. But the English veterinary doctor was the foremost and most strenuous of the Europeans to advocate passive surrender. His countenance actually turned pale and he trembled all over, whether from fear or the chilly atmosphere of the night I could not tell. Having heard from each one what he had to say, I could do nothing but step forward and speak to them, which I did in this wise: "Well, boys, you have all decided not to fight in case we are attacked, but to surrender our treasure. The ground for taking such a step is that we are sure to be outnumbered by a rebel host. So that in such a dilemma discretion is the better part of valor, and Tls. 40,000 are not worth sacrificing our lives for. But by surrendering our trust without making an effort of some kind to save it, we would be branded as unmitigated cowards, and we could never expect to be trusted with any responsible commission again. Now, I will tell you what I propose to do. If the rebel horde should come over and attempt to seize our treasure, I will spring forward with my yellow silk passport, and demand to see their chief, while you fellows with your guns and arms must stand by the treasure. Do not fire and start the fight. By parleying with them, it will for the moment check their determination to plunder, and they will have a chance to find out who we are, and where I obtained the passport; and, even if they should carry off the treasure, I shall tell their chief that I will surely report the whole proceeding in Nanking and recover every cent of our loss."

These remarks seemed to revive the spirit and courage of the men, after which we all sat on the forward decks of our boats anxiously waiting for what the next moment would bring forth. While in this state of expectancy, our hearts palpitating in an audible fashion, our eyes were watching intently the opposite shore. All the shouting and yelling seemed to have died away, and nothing could be seen but torches moving about slowly and leisurely in regular detachments, each detachment stopping occasionally and then moving on again. This was kept up for over two hours, while they constantly receded from us. I asked an old boatman the meaning of such movements and was told that the marauding horde was embarking in boats along the whole line of the opposite shore and was moving down stream. It was three o'clock in the morning, and it began to rain. A few of the advance boats had passed us without discovering where we were. They were loaded with men and floated by us in silence. By four o'clock the last boats followed the rest and soon disappeared from sight. Evidently, from the stillness that characterized the long line of boats as they floated down stream, the buccaneering horde was completely used up by their looting expedition, and at once abandoned themselves to sound sleep when they got on board the boats. We thanked our stars for such a narrow escape from such an unlooked-for danger. We owed our safety to the darkness of the night, the rain and to the fact that we were on the opposite shore in a retired cove. By five o'clock all our anxieties and fears were laid aside and turned into joy and thankfulness. We resumed our journey with light hearts and reached San Kow two days later in peace and safety. In less than two weeks we sent down to Wuhu, escorted by Europeans and tea-men, the first installment, consisting of fifteen boatloads of tea to be transhipped by steamer to Shanghai. The next installment consisted of twelve boatloads. I escorted that down the river in person. The river, in some places, especially in the summer, was quite shallow and a way had to be dug to float the boats down. In one or two instances the boatmen were very reluctant to jump into the water to do the work of deepening the river, and on one occasion I had to jump in, with the water up to my waist, in order to set them an example. When they caught the idea and saw me in the water, every man followed my example and vied with each other in clearing a way for the boats, for they saw I meant business and there was no fooling about it either.

I was engaged in this Taiping tea business for about six months, and took away about sixty-five thousand boxes of tea, which was hardly a tenth part of the entire stock found in the district. Then I was taken down with the fever and ague of the worst type. As I could get no medical relief at Wuhu, I was obliged to return to Shanghai, where I was laid up sick for nearly two months. Those two months of sickness had knocked all ideas of making a big fortune out of my head. I gave up the Taiping tea enterprise, because it called for a greater sacrifice of health and wear upon my nervous system than I was able to stand. The King Yuen midnight incident, which came near proving a disastrous one for me, with the marauding horde of unscrupulous cut-throats, had been quite a shock on my nervous system at the time and may have been the primal cause of my two months' sickness; it served as a sufficient warning to me not to tax my nervous system by further encounters and disputes with the rebel chiefs, whose price on the tea we bought of them was being increased every day. A dispassionate and calm view of the enterprise convinced me that I would have to preserve my life, strength and energy for a higher and worthier object than any fortune I might make out of this Taiping tea, which, after all, was plundered property. I am sure that no fortune in the world could be brought in the balance to weigh against my life, which is of inestimable value to me.

Although I had made nothing out of the Taiping teas, yet the fearless spirit, the determination to succeed, and the pluck to be able to do what few would undertake in face of exceptional difficulties and hazards, that I had exhibited in the enterprise, were in themselves assets worth more to me than a fortune. I was well-known, both among foreign merchants and native business men, so that as soon as it was known that I had given up the Taiping tea enterprise on account of health, I was offered a tea agency in the port of Kew Keang for packing teas for another foreign firm. I accepted it as a temporary shift, but gave it up in less than six months and started a commission business on my own account. I continued this business for nearly three years and was doing as well as I had expected to do. It was at this time while in Kew Keang that I caught the first ray of hope of materializing the educational scheme I had been weaving during the last year of my college life.

XIII

My Interviews with Tsang Kwoh Fan

In 1863, I was apparently prospering in my business, when, to my great surprise, an unexpected letter from the city of Ngan Khing, capital of An Whui province, was received. The writer was an old friend whose acquaintance I had made in Shanghai in 1857. He was a native of Ningpo, and was in charge of the first Chinese gunboat owned by the local Shanghai guild. He had apparently risen in official rank and had become one of Tsang Kwoh Fan's secretaries. His name was Chang Shi Kwei. In this letter, Chang said he was authorized by Viceroy Tsang Kwoh Fan to invite me to come down to Ngan Khing to call, as he (the Viceroy) had heard of me and wished very much to see me. On the receipt of the letter I was in a quandary and asked myself many questions: What could such a distinguished man want of me? Had he got wind of my late visit to Nanking and of my late enterprise to the district of Taiping for the green tea that was held there by the rebels? Tsang Kwoh Fan himself had been in the department of Hwui Chow fighting the rebels a year before and had been defeated, and he was reported to have been killed in battle. Could he have been told that I had been near the scene of his battle and had been in communication with the rebels, and did he want, under a polite invitation, to trap me and have my head off? But Chang, his secretary, was an old friend of many years' standing. I knew his character well; he wouldn't be likely to play the cat's paw to have me captured. Thus deliberating from one surmise to another, I concluded not to accept the invitation until I had learned more of the great man's purpose in sending for me.

In reply to the letter, I wrote and said I thanked His Excellency for his great condescension and considered it a great privilege and honor to be thus invited, but on account of the tea season having set in (which was in February), I was obliged to attend to the orders for packing tea that were fast coming in; but that as soon as they were off my hands, I would manage to go and pay my respects to His Excellency.

Two months after receiving the first letter, a second one came urging me to come to Ngan Khing as early as possible. This second letter enclosed a letter written by Li Sien Lan, the distinguished Chinese mathematician, whose acquaintance I had also made while in Shanghai. He was the man who assisted a Mr. Wiley, a missionary of the London Board of Missions, in the translation of several mathematical works into Chinese, among which was the Integral and Differential Calculus over which I well remember to have "flunked and fizzled" in my sophomore year in college; and, in this connection, I might as well frankly own that in my make-up mathematics was left out. Mr. Li Sien Lan was also an astronomer. In his letter, he said he had told Viceroy Tsang Kwoh Fan who I was and that I had had a foreign education; how I had raised a handsome subscription to help the famine refugees in 1857; that I had a strong desire to help China to become prosperous, powerful and strong. He said the viceroy had some important business for me to do, and that Chu and Wa, who were interested in machinery of all kinds, were also in Ngan Khing, having been invited there by the Viceroy. Mr. Li's letter completely dispelled all doubts and misgivings on my part as to the viceroy's design in wishing to see me, and gave me an insight as to his purpose for sending for me.

As an answer to these letters, I wrote saying that in a couple of months I should be more at liberty to take the journey. But my second reply did not seem to satisfy the strong desire on the part of Tsang Kwoh Fan to see me. So in July, 1863, I received a third letter from Chang and a second one from Li. In these letters the object of the viceroy was clearly and frankly stated. He wanted me to give up my mercantile business altogether and identify myself under him in the service of the state government, and asked whether or not I could come down to Ngan Khing at once. In view of this unexpected offer, which demanded prompt and explicit decision, I was not slow to see what possibility there was of carrying out my educational scheme, having such a powerful man as Tsang Kwoh Fan to back it. I immediately replied that upon learning the wishes of His Excellency, I had taken the whole situation into consideration, and had concluded to go to his headquarters at Ngan Khing, just as soon as I had wound up my business, which would take me a complete month, and that I would start by August at the latest. Thus ended the correspondence which was really the initiatory step of my official career.

Tsang Kwoh Fan was a most remarkable character in Chinese history. He was regarded by his contemporaries as a great scholar and a learned man. Soon after the Taiping Rebellion broke out and began to assume vast proportions, carrying before it province after province, Tsang began to drill an army of his own compatriots of Hunan who had always had the reputation of being brave and hardy fighters. In his work of raising a disciplined army, he secured the co-operation of other Hunan men, who afterwards took a prominent part in building up a flotilla of river gun-boats. This played a great and efficient part as an auxiliary force on the Yangtze River, and contributed in no small measure to check the rapid and ready concentration of the rebel forces, which had spread over a vast area on both banks of the great Yangtze River. In the space of a few years the lost provinces were gradually recovered, till the rebellion was narrowed down within the single province of Kiang Su, of which Nanking, the capital of the rebellion, was the only stronghold left. This finally succumbed to the forces of Tsang Kwoh Fan in 1864.

To crush and end a rebellion of such dimensions as that of the Taipings was no small task. Tsang Kwoh Fan was made the generalissimo of the imperialists. To enable him to cope successfully with the Taipings, Tsang was invested with almost regal power. The revenue of seven or eight provinces was laid at his feet for disposal, also official ranks and territorial appointments were at his command. So Tsang Kwoh Fan was literally and practically the supreme power of China at the time. But true to his innate greatness, he was never known to abuse the almost unlimited power that was placed in his hands, nor did he take advantage of the vast resources that were at his disposal to enrich himself or his family, relatives or friends. Unlike Li Hung Chang, his protégé and successor, who bequeathed Tls. 40,000,000 to his descendants after his death, Tsang died comparatively poor, and kept the escutcheon of his official career untarnished and left a name and character honored and revered for probity, patriotism and purity. He had great talents, but he was modest. He had a liberal mind, but he was conservative. He was a perfect gentleman and a nobleman of the highest type. It was such a man that I had the great fortune to come in contact with in the fall of 1863.

After winding up my business in New Keang, I took passage in a native boat and landed at Ngan Khing in September. There, in the military headquarters of Viceroy Tsang Kwoh Fan, I was met by my friends, Chang Si Kwei, Li Sien Lan, Wha Yuh Ting and Chu Siuh Chune, all old friends from Shanghai. They were glad to see me, and told me that the viceroy for the past six months, after hearing them tell that as a boy I had gone to America to get a Western education, had manifested the utmost curiosity and interest to see me, which accounted for the three letters which Chang and Li had written urging me to come. Now, since I had arrived, their efforts to get me there had not been fruitless, and they certainly claimed some credit for praising me up to the viceroy. I asked them if they knew what His Excellency wanted me for, aside from the curiosity of seeing a native of China made into a veritable Occidental. They all smiled significantly and told me that I would find out after one or two interviews. From this, I judged that they knew the object for which I was wanted by the Viceroy, and perhaps, they were at the bottom of the whole secret.

The next day I was to make my début, and called. My card was sent in, and without a moment's delay or waiting in the ante-room, I was ushered into the presence of the great man of China. After the usual ceremonies of greeting, I was pointed to a seat right in front of him. For a few minutes he sat in silence, smiling all the while as though he were much pleased to see me, but at the same time his keen eyes scanned me over from head to foot to see if he could discover anything strange in my outward appearance. Finally, he took a steady look into my eyes which seemed to attract his special attention. I must confess I felt quite uneasy all the while, though I was not abashed. Then came his first question.

"How long were you abroad?"

"I was absent from China eight years in pursuit of a Western education."

"Would you like to be a soldier in charge of a company?"

"I should be pleased to head one if I had been fitted for it. I have never studied military science."

"I should judge from your looks, you would make a fine soldier, for I can see from your eyes that you are brave and can command."

"I thank Your Excellency for the compliment. I may have the courage of a soldier, but I certainly lack military training and experience, and on that account I may not be able to meet Your Excellency's expectations."

When the question of being a soldier was suggested, I thought he really meant to have me enrolled as an officer in his army against the rebels; but in this I was mistaken, as my Shanghai friends told me afterwards. He simply put it forward to find out whether my mind was at all martially inclined. But when he found by my response that the bent of my thought was something else, he dropped the military subject and asked me my age and whether or not I was married. The last question closed my first introductory interview, which had lasted only about half an hour. He began to sip his tea and I did likewise, which according to Chinese official etiquette means that the interview is ended and the guest is at liberty to take his departure.

I returned to my room, and my Shanghai friends soon flocked around me to know what had passed between the viceroy and myself. I told them everything, and they were highly delighted.

Tsang Kwoh Fan, as he appeared in 1863, was over sixty years of age, in the very prime of life. He was five feet, eight or nine inches tall, strongly built and well-knitted together and in fine proportion. He had a broad chest and square shoulders surmounted by a large symmetrical head. He had a broad and high forehead; his eyes were set on a straight line under triangular-shaped eyelids, free from that obliquity so characteristic of the Mongolian type of countenance usually accompanied by high cheek bones, which is another feature peculiar to the Chinese physiognomy. His face was straight and somewhat hairy. He allowed his side whiskers their full growth; they hung down with his full beard which swept across a broad chest and added dignity to a commanding appearance. His eyes though not large were keen and penetrating. They were of a clear hazel color. His mouth was large but well compressed with thin lips which showed a strong will and a high purpose. Such was Tsang Kwoh Fan's external appearance, when I first met him at Ngan Khing.

Regarding his character, he was undoubtedly one of the most remarkable men of his age and time. As a military general, he might be called a self-made man; by dint of his indomitable persistence and perseverance, he rose from his high scholarship as a Hanlin (Chinese LL.D.) to be a generalissimo of all the imperial forces that were levied against the Taiping rebels, and in less than a decade after he headed his Hunan raw recruits, he succeeded in reducing the wide devastations of the rebellion that covered a territorial area of three of the richest provinces of China to the single one of Kiang Nan, till finally, by the constriction of his forces, he succeeded in crushing the life out of the rebellion by the fall and capture of Nanking. The Taiping Rebellion was of fifteen years' duration, from 1850 to 1865. It was no small task to bring it to its extinction. Its rise and progress had cost the Empire untold treasures, while 25,000,000 human lives were immolated in that political hecatomb. The close of the great rebellion gave the people a breathing respite. The Dowager Empress had special reasons to be grateful to the genius of Tsang Kwoh Fan, who was instrumental in restoring peace and order to the Manchu Dynasty. She was not slow, however, to recognize Tsang Kwoh Fan's merits and moral worth and created him a duke. But Tsang's greatness was not to be measured by any degree of conventional nobility; it did not consist in his victories over the rebels, much less in his re-capture of Nanking. It rose from his great virtues: his pure, unselfish patriotism, his deep and far-sighted statesmanship, and the purity of his official career. He is known in history as "the man of rectitude." This was his posthumous title conferred on him by imperial decree.

To resume the thread of my story, I was nearly two weeks in the viceroy's headquarters, occupying a suite of rooms in the same building assigned to my Shanghai friends—Li, Chang, Wha and Chu. There were living in his military headquarters at least two hundred officials, gathered there from all parts of the Empire, for various objects and purposes. Besides his secretaries, who numbered no less than a hundred, there were expectant officials, learned scholars, lawyers, mathematicians, astronomers and machinists; in short, the picked and noted men of China were all drawn there by the magnetic force of his character and great name. He always had a great admiration for men of distinguished learning and talents, and loved to associate and mingle with them. During the two weeks of my sojourn there, I had ample opportunity to call upon my Shanghai friends, and in that way incidentally found out what the object of the Viceroy was in urging me to be enrolled in the government service. It seemed that my friends had had frequent interviews with the Viceroy in regard to having a foreign machine shop established in China, but it had not been determined what kind of a machine shop should be established. One evening they gave me a dinner, at which time the subject of the machine shop was brought up and it became the chief topic. After each man had expressed his views on the subject excepting myself, they wanted to know what my views were, intimating that in all likelihood in my next interview with the Viceroy he would bring up the subject. I said that as I was not an expert in the matter, my opinions or suggestions might not be worth much, but nevertheless from my personal observation in the United States and from a common-sense point of view, I would say that a machine shop in the present state of China should be of a general and fundamental character and not one for specific purposes. In other words, I told them they ought to have a machine shop that would be able to create or reproduce other machine shops of the same character as itself; each and all of these should be able to turn out specific machinery for the manufacture of specific things. In plain words, they would have to have general and fundamental machinery in order to turn out specific machinery. A machine shop consisting of lathes of different kinds and sizes, planers and drills would be able to turn out machinery for making guns, engines, agricultural implements, clocks, etc. In a large country like China, I told them, they would need many primary or fundamental machine shops, but that after they had one (and a first-class one at that) they could make it the mother shop for reproducing others—perhaps better and more improved. If they had a number of them, it would enable them to have the shops co-operate with each other in case of need. It would be cheaper to have them reproduced and multiplied in China, I said, where labor and material were cheaper, than in Europe and America. Such was my crude idea of the subject. After I had finished, they were apparently much pleased and interested, and expressed the hope that I would state the same views to the Viceroy if he should ask me about the subject.

Several days after the dinner and conversation, the Viceroy did send for me. In this interview he asked me what in my opinion was the best thing to do for China at that time. The question came with such a force of meaning, that if I had not been forwarned by my friends a few evenings before, or if their hearts had not been set on the introduction of a machine shop, and they had not practically won the Viceroy over to their pet scheme, I might have been strongly tempted to launch forth upon my educational scheme as a reply to the question as to what was the best thing to do for China. But in such an event, being a stranger to the Viceroy, having been brought to his notice simply through the influence of my friends, I would have run a greater risk of jeopardizing my pet scheme of education than if I were left to act independently. My obligations to them were great, and I therefore decided that my constancy and fidelity to their friendship should be correspondingly great. So, instead of finding myself embarrassed in answering such a large and important question, I had a preconceived answer to give, which seemed to dove-tail into his views already crystallized into definite form, and which was ready to be carried out at once. So my educational scheme was put in the background, and the machine shop was allowed to take precedence. I repeated in substance what I had said to my friends previously in regard to establishing a mother machine shop, capable of reproducing other machine shops of like character, etc. I especially mentioned the manufacture of rifles, which, I said, required for the manufacture of their component parts separate machinery, but that the machine shop I would recommend was not one adapted for making the rifles, but adapted to turn out specific machinery for the making of rifles, cannons, cartridges, or anything else.

"Well," said he, "this is a subject quite beyond my knowledge. It would be well for you to discuss the matter with Wha and Chu, who are more familiar with it than I am and we will then decide what is best to be done."

This ended my interview with the Viceroy. After I left him, I met my friends, who were anxious to know the result of the interview. I told them of the outcome. They were highly elated over it. In our last conference it was decided that the matter of the character of the machine shop was to be left entirely to my discretion and judgment, after consulting a professional mechanical engineer. At the end of another two weeks, Wha was authorized to tell me that the Viceroy, after having seen all the four men, had decided to empower me to go abroad and make purchases of such machinery as in the opinion of a professional engineer would be the best and the right machinery for China to adopt. It was also left entirely to me to decide where the machinery should be purchased,— either in England, France or the United States of America.

The location of the machine shop was to be at a place called Kow Chang Meu, about four miles northwest of the city of Shanghai. The Kow Chang Meu machine shop was afterwards known as the Kiang Nan Arsenal, an establishment that covers several acres of ground and embraces under its roof all the leading branches of mechanical work. Millions have been invested in it since I brought the first machinery from Fitchburg, Mass., in order to make it one of the greatest arsenals east of the Cape of Good Hope. It may properly be regarded as a lasting monument to commemorate Tsang Kwoh Fan's broadmindedness as well as far-sightedness in establishing Western machinery in China.

XIV

My Mission to America to Buy Machinery

Aweek after my last interview with the Viceroy and after I had been told that I was to be entrusted with the execution of the order, my commission was made out and issued to me. In addition to the commission, the fifth official rank was conferred on me. It was a nominal civil rank, with the privilege of wearing the blue feather, as was customary only in war time and limited to those connected with the military service, but discarded in the civil service, where the peacock's feather is conferred only by imperial sanction. Two official despatches were also made out, directing me where to receive the Tls. 68,000, the entire amount for the purchase of the machinery. One-half of the amount was to be paid by the Taotai of Shanghai, and the other half by the Treasurer of Canton. After all the preliminary preparations had been completed, I bade farewell to the Viceroy and my Shanghai friends and started on my journey.

On my arrival in Shanghai in October, 1863, I had the good fortune to meet Mr. John Haskins, an American mechanical engineer, who came out to China with machinery for Messrs. Russell & Co. He had finished his business with that firm and was expecting soon to return to the States with his family—a wife and a little daughter. He was just the man I wanted. It did not take us long to get acquainted and as the time was short, we soon came to an understanding. We took the overland route from Hong Kong to London, via the Isthmus of Suez. Haskins and his family took passage on the French Messagerie Imperial line, while I engaged mine on board of one of the Peninsular & Oriental steamers. In my route to London, I touched at Singapore, crossed the Indian Ocean, and landed at Ceylon, where I changed steamers for Bengal up the Red Sea and landed at Cairo, where I had to cross the Isthmus by rail. The Suez Canal was not finished; the work of excavating was still going on. Arriving at Alexandria, I took passage from there to Marseilles, the southern port of France, while Haskins and his family took a steamer direct for Southampton. From Marseilles I went to Paris by rail. I was there about ten days, long enough to give me a general idea of the city, its public buildings, churches, gardens, and of Parisian gaiety. I crossed the English channel from Calais to Dover and went thence by rail to London—the first time in my life to touch English soil, and my first visit to the famous metropolis. While in London, I visited Whitworth's machine shop, and had the pleasure of renewing my acquaintance with Thomas Christy, whom I knew in China in the '50's. I was about a month in England, and then crossed the Atlantic in one of the Cunard steamers and landed in New York in the early spring of 1864, just ten years after my graduation from Yale and in ample time to be present at the decennial meeting of my class in July. Haskins and his family had preceded me in another steamer for New York, in order that he might get to work on the drawings and specifications of the shop and machinery and get them completed as soon as possble. In 1864, the last year of the great Civil War, nearly all the machine shops in the country, especially in New England, were preoccupied and busy in executing government orders, and it was very difficult to have my machinery taken up. Finally Haskins succeeded in getting the Putnam Machine Co., Fitchburg, Mass., to fill the order.

While Haskins was given sole charge of superintending the execution of the order, which required at least six months before the machinery could be completed for shipment to China, I took advantage of the interim to run down to New Haven and attend the decennial meeting of my class. It was to me a joyous event and I congratulated myself that I had the good luck to be present at our first re-union. Of course, the event that brought me back to the country was altogether unpretentious and had attracted little or no public attention at the time, because the whole country was completely engrossed in the last year of the great Civil War, yet I personally regarded my commission as an inevitable and preliminary step that would ultimately lead to the realization of my educational scheme, which had never for a moment escaped my mind. But at the meeting of my class, this subject of my life plan was not brought up. We had a most enjoyable time and parted with nearly the same fraternal feeling that characterized our parting at graduation. After the decennial meeting, I returned to Fitchburg and told Haskins that I was going down to Washington to offer my services to the government as a volunteer for the short period of six months, and that in case anything happened to me during the six months so that I could not come back to attend to the shipping of the machinery to Shanghai, he should attend to it. I left him all the papers—the cost and description of the machinery, the bills of lading, insurance, and freight, and directed him to send everything to the Viceroy's agent in Shanghai. This precautionary step having been taken, I slipped down to Washington.

Brigadier-General Barnes of Springfield, Mass., happened to be the general in charge of the Volunteer Department. His headquarters were at Willard's Hotel. I called on him and made known to him my object, that I felt as a naturalized citizen of the United States, it was my bounden duty to offer my services as a volunteer courier to carry despatches between Washington and the nearest Federal camp for at least six months, simply to show my loyalty and patriotism to my adopted country, and that I would furnish my own equipments. He said that he remembered me well, having met me in the Yale Library in New Haven, in 1853, on a visit to his son, William Barnes, who was in the college at the time I was, and who afterwards became a prominent lawyer in San Francisco. General Barnes asked what business I was engaged in. I told him that since my graduation in 1854 I had been in China and had recently returned with an order to purchase machinery for a machine shop ordered by Viceroy and Generalissimo Tsang Kwoh Fan. I told him the machinery was being made to order in Fitchburg, Mass., under the supervision of an American mechanical engineer, and as it would take at least six months before the same could be completed, I was anxious to offer my services to the government in the meantime as an evidence of my loyalty and patriotism to my adopted country. He was quite interested and pleased with what I said.

"Well, my young friend," said he, "I thank you very much for your offer, but since you are charged with a responsible trust to execute for the Chinese government, you had better return to Fitchburg to attend to it. We have plenty of men to serve, both as couriers and as fighting men to go to the front." Against this peremptory decision, I could urge nothing further, but I felt that I had at least fulfilled my duty to my adopted country.

XV

My Second Return to China

The machinery was not finished till the early spring of 1865. It was shipped direct from New York to Shanghai, China; while it was doubling the Cape of Good Hope on its way to the East, I took passage in another direction, back to China. I wanted to encircle the globe once in my life, and this was my opportunity. I could say after that, that I had circumnavigated the globe. So I planned to go back by way of San Francisco. In order to do that, I had to take into consideration the fact that the Union Pacific from Chicago to San Francisco via Omaha was not completed, nor was any steamship line subsidized by the United States government to cross the Pacific from San Francisco to any seaport, either in Japan or China at the time. On that account I was obliged to take a circuitous route, by taking a coast steamer from New York to Panama, cross the Isthmus, and from there take passage in another coast steamer up the Mexican coast to San Francisco, Cal.

At San Francisco, I was detained two weeks where I had to wait for a vessel to bridge me over the broad Pacific, either to Yokohama or Shanghai. At that time, as there was no other vessel advertised to sail for the East, I was compelled to take passage on board the "Ida de Rogers," a Nantucket bark. There were six passengers, including myself. We had to pay $500 each for passage from San Francisco to Yokohama. The crew consisted of the captain, who had with him his wife, and a little boy six years old, a mate, three sailors and a cook, a Chinese boy. The "Ida de Rogers" was owned by Captain Norton who hailed from Nantucket. She was about one hundred and fifty feet long—an old tub at that. She carried no cargo and little or no ballast, except bilge-water, which may have come from Nantucket, for aught I know. The skipper, true to the point of the country where they produce crops of seamen of microscopic ideas, was found to be not at all deficient in his close calculations of how to shave closely in every bargain and, in fact, in everything in life. In this instance, we had ample opportunity to find out under whom we were sailing. Before we were fairly out of the "Golden Gate," we were treated every day with salted mackerel, which

I took to be the daily and fashionable dish of Nantucket. The cook we had made matters worse, as he did not seem to know his business and was no doubt picked up in San Francisco just to fill the vacancy. The mackerel was cooked and brought on the table without being freshened, and the Indian meal cakes that were served with it, were but half baked, so that day after day we practically all left the table disgusted and half starved. Not only was the food bad and unhealthy, but the skipper's family was of a very low type. The skipper himself was a most profane man, and although I never heard the wife swear, yet she seemed to enjoy her husband's oaths. Their little boy who was not more than six years old, seemed to have surpassed the father in profanity. It may be said that the young scamp had mastered his shorter and longer catechism of profanity completely, for he was not wanting in expressions of the most disgusting and repulsive kind, as taught him by his sire, yet his parents sat listening to him with evident satisfaction, glancing around at the passengers to catch their approval. One of the passengers, an Englishman, who stood near listening and smoking his pipe, only remarked ironically, "You have a smart boy there." At this the skipper nodded, while the mother seemed to gloat over her young hopeful. Such a scene was of daily occurrence, and one that we could not escape, since we were cooped up in such narrow quarters on account of the smallness of the vessel. There was not even a five-foot deck where one could stretch his legs. We were most of the time shut up in the dining room, as it was the coolest spot we could find. Before our voyage was half over, we had occasion to land at one of the most northerly islands of the Hawaiian group for fresh water and provisions. While the vessel was being victualed, all the passengers landed and went out to the country to take a stroll, which was a great relief. We were gone nearly all day. We all re-embarked early in the evening. It seemed that the captain had filled the forward hold with chickens and young turkeys. We congratulated ourselves that the skipper after all had swung round to show a generous streak, which had only needed an opportunity to show itself, and that for the rest of the voyage he was no doubt going to feed us on fresh chickens and turkeys to make up for the salted mackerel, which might have given us the scurvy had we continued on the same diet. For the first day or so, after we resumed our voyage, we had chicken and fish for our breakfast and dinners, but that was the last we saw of the fresh provisions. We saw no turkey on the table. On making inquiry, the cook told us that both the chickens and the turkeys were bought, not for our table, but for speculation, to be sold on arrival in Yokohama. Unfortunately for the skipper, the chickens and turkeys for want of proper food and fresh air, had died a few days before our arrival at the port.

Immediately upon reaching Yokohama, I took passage in a P. & O. steamer for Shanghai.

On my arrival there, I found the machinery had all arrived a month before; it had all been delivered in good condition and perfect working order. I had been absent from China a little over a year. During that time Viceroy Tsang Kwoh Fan, with the co-operation of his brother, Tsang Kwoh Chuen, succeeded in the capture of Nanking, which put an end to the great Taiping Rebellion of 1850.

On my arrival in Shanghai, I found that the Viceroy had gone up to Chu Chow, the most northerly department of Kiangsu province, close to the border line of Shan Tung, and situated on the canal. He made that his headquarters in superintending the subjugation of the Nienfi or Anwhui rebels, against whom Li Hung Chang had been appointed as his lieutenant in the field. I was requested to go up to Chu Chow to make a report in person regarding the purchase of the machinery.

On my journey to Chu Chow, I was accompanied by my old friend Wha Yuh Ting part of the way. We went by the Grand Canal from Sinu-Mew at the Yangtze up as far as Yang Chow, the great entrepôt for the Government Salt Monopoly. There we took mule carts overland to Chu Chow. We were three days on our journey. Chu Chow is a departmental city and here, as stated before, Viceroy Tsang made his quarters. I was there three days. The Viceroy complimented me highly for what I had done. He made my late commission to the States to purchase machinery the subject of a special memorial to the government. Such a special memorial on any political event invariably gives it political prominence and weight, and in order to lift me at once from a position of no importance to a territorial civil appointment of the bona fide fifth rank, was a step seldom asked for or conceded. He made out my case to be an exceptional one, and the following is the language he used in his memorial:

"Yung Wing is a foreign educated Chinese. He has mastered the English language. In his journey over thousands of miles of ocean to the extreme ends of the earth to fulfill the commission I entrusted to him, he was utterly oblivious to difficulties and dangers that lay in his way. In this respect even the missions of the Ancients present no parallel equal to his. Therefore, I would recommend that he be promoted to the expectancy of one of the Kiangsu subprefects, and he is entitled to fill the first vacancy presenting itself, in recognition of his valuable services."

His secretary, who drew up the memorial at his dictation, gave me a copy of the memorial before I left Chu Chow for Shanghai, and congratulated me on the great honor the Viceroy had conferred on me. I thanked the Viceroy before bidding him good-bye, and expressed the hope that my actions in the future would justify his high opinion of me.

In less than two months after leaving him, an official document from the Viceroy reached me in Shanghai, and in October, 1865, I was a full-fledged mandarin of the fifth rank. While waiting as an expectant subprefect, I was retained by the provincial authorities as a government interpreter and translator. My salary was $250 per month. No other expectant official of the province—not even an expectant Taotai (an official of the fourth rank)—could command such a salary.

Ting Yih Chang was at the time Taotai of Shanghai. He and I became great friends. He rose rapidly in official rank and became successively salt commissioner, provincial treasurer and Taotai or governor of Kiang Nan. Through him, I also rose in official rank and was decorated with the peacock's feather. While Ting Yih Chang was salt commissioner, I accompanied him to Yang Chow and was engaged in translating Colton's geography into Chinese, for about six months. I then returned to Shanghai to resume my position as government interpreter and translator. I had plenty of time on my hands. I took to translating "Parsons on Contracts," which I thought might be useful to the Chinese. In this work I was fortunate in securing the services of a Chinese scholar to help me. I found him well versed in mathematics and in all Chinese official business, besides being a fine Chinese scholar and writer. He finally persuaded me not to continue the translation, as there was some doubt as to whether such a work, even when finished, would be in demand, because the Chinese courts are seldom troubled with litigations on contracts, and in all cases of violation of contracts, the Chinese code is used.

In 1867, Viceroy Tsang Kwoh Fan, with Li Hung Chang's co-operation, succeeded in ending the Nienfi rebellion, and came to Nanking to fill his viceroyalty of the two Kiangs.

Before taking up his position as viceroy of the Kiangs permanently, he took a tour of inspection through his jurisdiction and one of the important places he visited was Shanghai and the Kiang Nan Arsenal—an establishment of his own creation. He went through the arsenal with undisguised interest. I pointed out to him the machinery which I bought for him in America. He stood and watched its automatic movement with unabated delight, for this was the first time he had seen machinery, and how it worked. It was during this visit that I succeeded in persuading him to have a mechanical school annexed to the arsenal, in which Chinese youths might be taught the theory as well as the practice of mechanical engineering, and thus enable China in time to dispense with the employment of foreign mechanical engineers and machinists, and to be perfectly independent. This at once appealed to the practical turn of the Chinese mind, and the school was finally added to the arsenal. They are doubtless turning out at the present time both mechanical engineers and machinists of all descriptions.

XVI

Proposal of My Educational Scheme

Having scored in a small way this educational victory, by inducing the Viceroy to establish a mechanical training school as a corollary to the arsenal, I felt quite worked up and encouraged concerning my educational scheme which had been lying dormant in my mind for the past fifteen years, awaiting an opportunity to be brought forward.

Besides Viceroy Tsang Kwoh Fan, whom I counted upon to back me in furthering the scheme, Ting Yih Chang, an old friend of mine, had become an important factor to be reckoned with in Chinese politics. He was a man of progressive tendencies and was alive to all practical measures of reform. He had been appointed governor of Kiangsu province, and after his accession to his new office, I had many interviews with him regarding my educational scheme, in which he was intensely interested. He told me that he was in correspondence with Wen Seang, the prime minister of China, who was a Manchu, and that if I were to put my scheme in writing, he would forward it to Peking, and ask Wen Seang to use his influence to memorialize the government for its adoption. Such an unexpected piece of information came like a clap of thunder and fairly lifted me off my feet. I immediately left Suchau for Shanghai. With the help of my Nanking friend, who had helped me in the work of translating "Parsons on Contracts," I drew up four proposals to be presented to Governor Ting, to be forwarded by him to Minister Wen Seang, at Peking. They were as follows:

First Proposal

The first proposal contemplated the organization of a Steamship Company on a joint stock basis. No foreigner was to be allowed to be a stockholder in the company. It was to be a purely Chinese company, managed and worked by Chinese exclusively.

To insure its stability and success, an annual government subsidy was to be made in the shape of a certain percentage of the tribute rice carried to Peking from Shanghai and Chinkiang, and elsewhere, where tribute rice is paid over to the government in lieu of taxes in money. This tribute rice heretofore had been taken to Peking by flat-bottom boats, via the Grand Canal. Thousands of these boats were built expressly for this rice transportation, which supported a large population all along the whole route of the Grand Canal.

On account of the great evils arising from this mode of transportation, such as the great length of time it took to take the rice to Peking, the great percentage of loss from theft, and from fermentation, which made the rice unfit for food, part of the tribute rice was carried by sea in Ningpo junks as far as Tiensin, and from thence transhipped again in flat-bottom boats to Peking. But even the Ningpo junk system was attended with great loss of time and much damage, almost as great as by flat-bottom scows. My proposition was to use steam to do the work, supplanting both the flat-bottomed scows and the Ningpo junk system, so that the millions who were dependent on rice for subsistence might find it possible to get good and sound rice. This is one of the great benefits and blessings which the China Merchant Steamship Co. has conferred upon China.

Second Proposal

THE SECOND PROPOSITION WAS FOR the government to send picked Chinese youths abroad to be thoroughly educated for the public service. The scheme contemplated the education of one hundred and twenty students as an experiment. These one hundred and twenty students were to be divided into four installments of thirty students each, one installment to be sent out each year. They were to have fifteen years to finish their education. Their average age was to be from twelve to fourteen years. If the first and second installments proved to be a success, the scheme was to be continued indefinitely. Chinese teachers were to be provided to keep up their knowledge of Chinese while in the United States. Over the whole enterprise two commissioners were to be appointed, and the government was to appropriate a certain percentage of the Shanghai customs to maintain the mission.

Third Proposal

THE THIRD PROPOSITION WAS TO induce the government to open the mineral resources of the country and thus in an indirect way lead to the necessity of introducing railroads to transport the mineral products from the interior to the ports.

I did not expect this proposition to be adopted and carried out, because China at that time had no mining engineers who could be depended upon to develop the mines, nor were the people free from the Fung Shui superstition.[1] I had no faith whatever in the success of this proposition, but simply put it in writing to show how ambitious I was to have the government wake up to the possibilities of the development of its vast resources.

Fourth Proposal

THE ENCROACHMENT OF FOREIGN POWERS upon the independent sovereignty of China has always been watched by me with the most intense interest. No one who is at all acquainted with Roman Catholicism can fail to be impressed with the unwarranted pretensions and assumptions of the Romish church in China. She claims civil jurisdiction over her proselytes, and takes civil and criminal cases out of Chinese courts. In order to put a stop to such insidious and crafty workings to gain temporal power in China, I put forth this proposition: to prohibit missionaries of any religious sect or denomination from exercising any kind of jurisdiction over their converts, in either civil or criminal cases. These four propositions were carefully drawn up, and were presented to Governor Ting for transmission to Peking.

OF THE FOUR PROPOSALS, THE first, third and fourth were put in to chaperone the second, in which my whole heart was enlisted, and which above all others was the one I wanted to be taken up; but not to give it too prominent a place, at the suggestion of my Chinese teacher, it was assigned a second place in the order of the arrangement. Governor Ting recognized this, and accordingly wrote to Prime Minister Wen Seang and forwarded the proposals to Peking. Two months later, a letter from Ting, at Suchau, his headquarters, gave me to understand that news from Peking had reached him that Wen Seang's mother had died, and he was obliged, according to Chinese laws and customs, to retire from office and go into mourning for a period of twenty-seven

---

1. The doctrine held by the Chinese in relation to the spirits or genii that rule over winds and waters, especially running streams and subterranean waters. This doctrine is universal and inveterate among the Chinese, and in a great measure prompts their hostility to railroads and telegraphs, since they believe that such structures anger the spirits of the air and waters and consequently cause floods and typhoons.—*Standard Dictionary*.

months, equivalent to three years, and to abstain altogether from public affairs of all kinds. This news threw a cold blanket over my educational scheme for the time being. No sooner had one misfortune happened than another took its place, worst than the first—Wen Seang himself, three months afterwards, was overtaken by death during his retirement. This announcement appeared in the Peking "Gazette," which I saw, besides being officially informed of it by Governor Ting. No one who had a pet scheme to promote or a hobby to ride could feel more blue than I did, when the cup of joy held so near to his lips was dashed from him. I was not entirely disheartened by such circumstances, but had an abiding faith that my educational scheme would in the end come out all right. There was an interval of at least three years of suspense and waiting between 1868 and 1870. I kept pegging at Governor Ting, urging him to keep the subject constantly before Viceroy Tsang's mind. But like the fate of all measures of reform, it had to abide its time and opportunity.

The time and the opportunity for my educational scheme to materialize finally came. Contrary to all human expectations, the opportunity appeared in the guise of the Tientsin Massacre. No more did Samson, when he slew the Timnath lion, expect to extract honey from its carcass than did I expect to extract from the slaughter of the French nuns and Sisters of Charity the educational scheme that was destined to make a new China of the old, and to work out an Oriental civilization on an Occidental basis.

The Tientsin Massacre took place early in 1870. It arose from the gross ignorance and superstition of the Tientsin populace regarding the work of the nuns and Sisters of Charity, part of whose religious duty it was to rescue foundlings and castaway orphans, who were gathered into hospitals, cared for and educated for the services of the Roman Catholic church. This beneficent work was misunderstood and misconstrued by the ignorant masses, who really believed in the rumors and stories that the infants and children thus gathered in were taken into the hospitals and churches to have their eyes gouged out for medical and religious purposes. Such diabolical reports soon spread like wild-fire till popular excitement was worked up to its highest pitch of frenzy, and the infuriated mob, regardless of death and fearless of law, plunged headlong into the Tientsin Massacre. In that massacre a Protestant church was burned and destroyed, as was also a Roman Catholic church and hospital; several nuns or Sisters of Charity were killed.

At the time of this occurrence, Chung Hou was viceroy of the Metropolitan province. He had been ambassador to Russia previously, but in this unfortunate affair, according to Chinese law, he was held responsible, was degraded from office and banished. The whole imbroglio was finally settled and patched up by the payment of an indemnity to the relatives and friends of the victims of the massacre and the rebuilding of the Roman Catholic and Protestant churches, another Catholic hospital, besides a suitable official apology made by the government for the incident. Had the French government not been handicapped by the impending German War which threatened her at the time, France would certainly have made the Tientsin Massacre a *casus belli*, and another slice of the Chinese Empire would have been annexed to the French possessions in Asia. As it was, Tonquin, a tributary state of China, was afterwards unscrupulously wrenched from her.

In the settlement of the massacre, the Imperial commissioners appointed were: Viceroy Tsang Kwoh Fan, Mow Chung Hsi, Liu * * * and Ting Yih Chang, Governor of Kiang Su. Li Hung Chang was still in the field finishing up the Nienfi rebellion, otherwise he, too, would have been appointed to take part in the proceedings of the settlement. I was telegraphed for by my friend, Ting Yih Chang, to be present to act as interpreter on the occasion, but the telegram did not reach me in time for me to accompany him to Tientsin; but I reached Tientsin in time to witness the last proceedings. The High Commissioners, after the settlement with the French, for some reason or other, did not disband, but remained in Tientsin for several days. They evidently had other matters of State connected with Chung Hou's degradation and banishment to consider.

XVII

The Chinese Educational Mission

T aking advantage of their presence, I seized the opportunity to press my educational scheme upon the attention of Ting Yih Chang and urged him to present the subject to the Board of Commissioners of which Tsang Kwoh Fan was president. I knew Ting sympathized with me in the scheme, and I knew, too, that Tsang Kwoh Fan had been well informed of it three years before through Governor Ting. Governor Ting took up the matter in dead earnest and held many private interviews with Tsang Kwoh Fan as well as with the other members of the Commission. One evening, returning to his headquarters very late, he came to my room and awakened me and told me that Viceroy Tsang and the other Commissioners had unanimously decided to sign their names conjointly in a memorial to the government to adopt my four propositions. This piece of news was too much to allow me to sleep any more that night; while lying on my bed, as wakeful as an owl, I felt as though I were treading on clouds and walking in air. Two days after this stirring piece of news, the memorial was jointly signed with Viceroy Tsang Kwoh Fan's name heading the list, and was on its way to Peking by pony express. Meanwhile, before the Board of Commissioners disbanded and Viceroy Tsang took his departure for Nanking, it was decided that Chin Lan Pin, a member of the Hanlin College, who had served twenty years as a clerk in the Board of Punishment, should be recommended by Ting to co-operate with me in charge of the Chinese Educational Commission. The ground upon which Chin Lan Pin was recommended as a co-commissioner was that he was a Han Lin and a regularly educated Chinese, and the enterprise would not be so likely to meet with the opposition it might have if I were to attempt to carry it out alone, because the scheme in principle and significance was against the Chinese theory of national education, and it would not have taken much to create a reaction to defeat the plan on account of the intense conservatism of the government. The wisdom and the shrewd policy of such a move appealed to me at once, and I accepted the suggestion with pleasure and alacrity. So Chin Lan Pin was written to and came to Tientsin. The next day, after a farewell dinner had been accorded to the

Board of Commissioners before it broke up, Governor Ting introduced me to Chin Lan Pin, whom I had never met before and who was to be my associate in the educational scheme. He evidently was pleased to quit Peking, where he had been cooped up in the Board of Punishment for twenty years as a clerk. He had never filled a government position in any other capacity in his life, nor did he show any practical experience in the world of business and hard facts. In his habits he was very retiring, but very scholarly. In disposition he was kindly and pleasant, but very timid and afraid of responsibilities of even a feather's weight.

In the winter of 1870, Tsang Kwoh Fan, after having settled the Tientsin imbroglio, returned to Nanking, his headquarters as the viceroy of the two Kiangs. There he received the imperial rescript sanctioning his joint memorial on the four proposals submitted through Ting Yih Chang for adoption by the government. He notified me on the subject. It was a glorious piece of news, and the Chinese educational project thus became a veritable historical fact, marking a new era in the annals of China. Tsang invited me to repair to Nanking, and during that visit the most important points connected with the mission were settled, viz.: the establishment of a preparatory school; the number of students to be selected to be sent abroad; where the money was to come from to support the students while there; the number of years they were to be allowed to remain there for their education.

The educational commission was to consist of two commissioners, Chin Lan Pin and myself. Chin Lan Pin's duty was to see that the students should keep up their knowledge of Chinese while in America; my duty was to look after their foreign education and to find suitable homes for them. Chin Lan Pin and myself were to look after their expenses conjointly. Two Chinese teachers were provided to keep up their studies in Chinese, and an interpreter was provided for the Commission. Yeh Shu Tung and Yung Yune Foo were the Chinese teachers and Tsang Lai Sun was the interpreter. Such was the composition of the Chinese Educational Commission.

As to the character and selection of the students: the whole number to be sent abroad for education was one hundred and twenty; they were to be divided into four installments of thirty members each, one installment to be sent each year for four successive years at about the same time. The candidates to be selected were not to be younger than twelve or older than fifteen years of age. They were to show respectable parentage or responsible and respectable guardians. They were required to pass a medical examination, and an examination in their Chinese studies according to regulation—reading and writing in Chinese—also to pass an English examination if a candidate had been in an English school. All successful candidates were required to repair every day to the preparatory school, where teachers were provided to continue with their Chinese studies, and to begin the study of English or to continue with their English studies, for at least one year before they were to embark for the United States.

Parents and guardians were required to sign a paper which stated that without recourse, they were perfectly willing to let their sons or protégés go abroad to be educated for a period of fifteen years, from the time they began their studies in the United States until they had finished, and that during the fifteen years, the government was not to be responsible for death or for any accident that might happen to any student.

The government guaranteed to pay all their expenses while they were being educated. It was to provide every installment with a Chinese teacher to accompany it to the United States, and to give each installment of students a suitable outfit. Such were the requirements and the organization of the student corps.

Immediately upon my return to Shanghai from Nanking after my long interview with the Viceroy, my first step was to have a preparatory school established in Shanghai for the accommodation of at least thirty students, which was the full complement for the first installment. Liu Kai Sing, who was with the Viceroy for a number of years as his first secretary in the Department on Memorials, was appointed superintendent of the preparatory school in Shanghai. In him, I found an able coadjutor as well as a staunch friend who took a deep interest in the educational scheme. He it was who prepared all the four installments of students to come to this country.

Thus the China end of the scheme was set afloat in the summer of 1871. To make up the full complement of the first installment of students, I had to take a trip down to Hong Kong to visit the English government schools to select from them a few bright candidates who had had some instruction both in English and Chinese studies. As the people in the northern part of China did not know that such an educational scheme had been projected by the government, there being no Chinese newspapers published at that time to spread the news among the people, we had, at first, few applications for entrance into the preparatory school. All the applications came from the Canton people, especially from the district of Heang Shan. This accounts for the fact that nine-tenths of the one hundred and twenty government students were from the south.

In the winter of 1871, a few months after the preparatory school had begun operations, China suffered an irreparable loss by the death of Viceroy Tsang Kwoh Fan, who died in Nanking at the ripe age of seventy-one years. Had his life been spared even a year longer, he would have seen the first installment of thirty students started for the United States,—the first fruit of his own planting. But founders of all great and good works are not permitted by the nature and order of things to live beyond their ordained limitations to witness the successful developments of their own labor in this world; but the consequences of human action and human character, when once their die is cast, will reach to eternity. Sufficient for Tsang Kwoh Fan that he had completed his share in the educational line well. He did a great and glorious work for China and posterity, and those who were privileged to reap the benefit of his labor will find ample reason to bless him as China's great benefactor. Tsang, as a statesman, a patriot, and as a man, towered above his contemporaries even as Mount Everest rises above the surrounding heights of the Himalaya range, forever resting in undisturbed calmness and crowned with the purity of everlasting snow. Before he breathed his last, I was told that it was his wish that his successor and protégé, Li Hung Chang, be requested to take up his mantle and carry on the work of the Chinese Educational Commission.

Li Hung Chang was of an altogether different make-up from his distinguished predecessor and patron. He was of an excitable and nervous temperament, capricious and impulsive, susceptible to flattery and praise, or, as the Chinese laconically put it, he was fond of wearing tall hats. His outward manners were brusque, but he was inwardly kind-hearted. As a statesman he was far inferior to Tsang; as a patriot and politician, his character could not stand a moment before the searchlight of cold and impartial history. It was under such a man that the Chinese Educational Commission was launched forth.

In the latter part of the summer of 1872 the first installment of Chinese students, thirty in number, were ready to start on the passage across the Pacific to the United States. In order that they might have homes to go to on their arrival, it devolved upon me to precede them by one month, leaving Chin Lan Pin, the two Chinese teachers and their interpreter to come on a mail later. After reaching New York by the Baltimore and Ohio, via Washington, I went as far as New Haven on my way to Springfield, Mass., where I intended to meet the students and other members of the commission on their way to the East by the Boston and Albany Railroad. At New Haven, the first person I called upon to announce my mission was Prof. James Hadley. He was indeed glad to see me, and was delighted to know that I had come back with such a mission in my hands. After making my wants known to him, he immediately recommended me to call upon Mr. B. G. Northrop, which I did. Mr. Northrop was then Commissioner of Education for Connecticut. I told him my business and asked his advice. He strongly recommended me to distribute and locate the students in New England families, either by twos or fours to each family, where they could be cared for and at the same time instructed, till they were able to join classes in graded schools. This advice I followed at once. I went on to Springfield, Mass., which city I considered was the most central point from which to distribute the students in New England; for this reason I chose Springfield for my headquarters. This enabled me to be very near my friends, Dr. A. S. McClean and his worthy wife, both of whom had been my steadfast friends since 1854.

But through the advice of Dr. B. G. Northrop and other friends, I made my permanent headquarters in the city of Hartford, Conn., and for nearly two years our headquarters were located on Sumner Street. I did not abandon Springfield, but made it the center of distribution and location of the students as long as they continued to come over, which was for three successive years, ending in 1875.

In 1874, Li Hung Chang, at the recommendation of the commission, authorized me to put up a handsome, substantial building on Collins Street as the permanent headquarters of the Chinese Educational Commission in the United States. In January, 1875, we moved into our new headquarters, which was a large, double three-story house spacious enough to accommodate the Commissioners, teachers and seventy-five students at one time. It was provided with a school-room where Chinese was exclusively taught; a dining room, a double kitchen, dormitories and bath rooms. The motive which led me to build permanent headquarters of our own was to have the educational mission as deeply rooted in the United States as possible, so as not to give the Chinese government any chance of retrograding in this movement. Such was my proposal, but that was not God's disposal as subsequent events plainly proved.

XVIII

INVESTIGATION OF THE COOLIE TRAFFIC IN PERU

In the spring of 1873, I returned to China on a flying visit for the sole purpose of introducing the Gatling gun—a comparatively new weapon of warfare of a most destructive character. I had some difficulty in persuading the Gatling Company to give me the sole agency of the gun in China, because they did not know who I was, and were unacquainted with my practical business experience. In fact, they did not know how successfully I had carried on the Taiping Green Tea Expedition in 1860–1, in the face of dangers and privations which few men dared to face. However, I prevailed on the president of the company, Dr. Gatling himself, the inventor of the gun, to entrust me with the agency. Exactly a month after my arrival in Tientsin, I cabled the company an order for a battery of fifty guns, which amounted altogether to something over $100,000, a pretty big order for a man who it was thought could not do anything. This order was followed by subsequent orders. I was anxious that China should have the latest modern guns as well as the latest modern educated men. The Gatling Company was satisfied with my work and had a different opinion of me afterwards.

While I was in Tientsin, attending to the gun business, the Viceroy told me that the Peruvian commissioner was there waiting to make a treaty with China regarding the further importation of coolie labor into Peru. He wanted me to call on the commissioner and talk with him on the subject, which I did. In his conversation, he pictured to me in rosy colors how well the Chinese were treated in Peru; how they were prospering and doing well there, and said that the Chinese government ought to conclude a treaty with Peru to encourage the poorer class of Chinese to emigrate to that country, which offered a fine chance for them to better themselves. I told him that I knew something about the coolie traffic as it was carried on in Macao; how the country people were inveigled and kidnapped, put into barracoons and kept there by force till they were shipped on board, where they were made to sign labor contracts either for Cuba or Peru. On landing at their destination, they were then sold to the highest bidder, and made to sign another contract with their new

YUNG WING

masters, who took special care to have the contract renewed at the end of every term, practically making slaves of them for life. Then I told him something about the horrors of the middle passage between Macao and Cuba or Peru; how whole cargoes of them revolted in mid-ocean, and either committed wholesale suicide by jumping into the ocean, or else overpowered the captain and the crew, killed them and threw them overboard, and then took their chances in the drifting of the vessel.

Such were some of the facts and horrors of the coolie traffic I pictured to the Peruvian Commissioner. I told him plainly that he must not expect me to help him in this diabolical business. On the contrary, I told him I would dissuade the Viceroy from entering into a treaty with Peru to carry on such inhuman traffic. How the Peruvian's countenance changed when he heard me deliver my mind on the subject! Disappointment, displeasure and anger were visible in his countenance. I bade him good morning, for I was myself somewhat excited as I narrated what I had seen in Macao and what I had read in the papers about the coolie traffic. Indeed, one of the first scenes I had seen on my arrival in Macao in 1855 was a string of poor Chinese coolies tied to each other by their cues and led into one of the barracoons like abject slaves. Once, while in Canton, I had succeeded in having two or three kidnappers arrested, and had them put into wooden collars weighing forty pounds, which the culprits had to carry night and day for a couple of months as a punishment for their kidnapping.

Returning to the Viceroy, I told him I had made the call, and narrated my interview. The Viceroy, to make my visit short, then said, "You have come back just in time to save me from cabling you. I wish you to return to Hartford as quickly as possible and make preparations to proceed to Peru at once, to look into the condition of the Chinese coolies there."

On my return to Hartford, I found that Chin Lan Pin had also been instructed by the government to look after the condition of the Chinese coolies in Cuba. These collateral or side missions were ordered at Li Hung Chang's suggestion. I started on my mission before Chin Lan Pin did. My friend, the Rev. J. H. Twichell, and Dr. E. W. Kellogg, who afterwards became my brother-in-law, accompanied me on my trip. I finished my work inside of three months, and had my report completed before Chin started on his journey to Cuba. On his return, both of our reports were forwarded to Viceroy Li, who was in charge of all foreign diplomatic affairs.

My report was accompanied with two dozen photographs of Chinese coolies, showing how their backs had been lacerated and torn, scarred and disfigured by the lash. I had these photographs taken in the night, unknown to anyone except the victims themselves, who were, at my request, collected and assembled together for the purpose. I knew that these photographs would tell a tale of cruelty and inhumanity perpetrated by the owners of haciendas, which would be beyond cavil and dispute.

The Peruvian Commissioner, who was sent out to China to negotiate a treaty with Viceroy Li Hung Chang to continue the coolie traffic to Peru, was still in Tientsin waiting for the arrival of my report. A friend of mine wrote me that he had the hardihood to deny the statements in my report, and said that they could not be supported by facts. I had written to the Viceroy beforehand that he should hold the photographs in reserve, and keep them in the background till the Peruvian had exhausted all his arguments, and then produce them. My correspondent wrote me that the Viceroy followed my suggestion, and the photographs proved to be so incontrovertible and palpable that the Peruvian was taken by surprise and was dumbfounded. He retired completely crestfallen.

Since our reports on the actual conditions of Chinese coolies in Cuba and Peru were made, no more coolies have been allowed to leave China for those countries. The traffic had received its death blow.

XIX

End of the Educational Mission

In the fall of 1875 the last installment of students arrived. They came in charge of a new commissioner, Ou Ngoh Liang, two new Chinese teachers and a new interpreter, Kwang Kee Cheu. These new men were appointed by Viceroy Li Hung Chang. I knew them in China, especially the new commissioner and the interpreter.

These changes were made at the request of Chin Lan Pin, who expected soon to return to China on a leave of absence. He was going to take with him the old Chinese teacher, Yeh Shu Tung, who had rendered him great and signal service in his trip to Cuba on the coolie question the year before. Tsang Lai Sun, the old interpreter, was also requested to resign and returned to China. These changes I had anticipated some time before and they did not surprise me.

Three months after Chin Lan Pin's arrival in Peking, word came from China that he and I were appointed joint Chinese ministers to Washington, and that Yeh Shu Tung, the old Chinese teacher, was appointed secretary to the Chinese Legation. This was great news to me to be sure, but I did not feel ecstatic over it; on the contrary, the more I reflected on it, the more I felt depressed. But my friends who congratulated me on the honor and promotion did not take in the whole situation as it loomed up before my mind in all its bearings. As far as I was concerned, I had every reason to feel grateful and honored, but how about my life work—the Chinese educational mission that I had in hand—and which needed in its present stage great watchfulness and care? If, as I reflected, I were to be removed to Washington, who was there left behind to look after the welfare of the students with the same interest that I had manifested? It would be like separating the father from his children. This would not do, so I sat down and wrote to the Viceroy a letter, the tenor of which ran somewhat as follows: I thanked him for the appointment which I considered to be a great honor for any man to receive from the government; and said that while I appreciated fully its significance, the obligations and responsibilities inseparably connected with the position filled me with anxious solicitude that my abilities and qualifications might not be equal to their satisfactory fulfilment. In view of such a state of mind, I much preferred, if I were allowed to have my preference in the matter, to remain in my present position as a commissioner of the Chinese mission in Hartford and to continue in it till the Chinese students should have finished their education and were ready to return to China to serve the State in their various capacities. In that event I should have discharged a duty to "Tsang the Upright," and at the same time fulfilled a great duty to China. As Chin Lan Pin had been appointed minister at the same time, he would doubtless be able alone to meet the expectations of the government in his diplomatic capacity.

The letter was written and engrossed by Yung Yune Foo, one of the old Chinese teachers who came over with the first installment of students at the same time Yeh Shu Tung came. In less than four months an answer was received which partially acceded to my request by making me an assistant or associate minister, at the same time allowing me to retain my position as Commissioner of Education, and in that capacity, to exercise a general supervision over the education of the students.

Ou Ngoh Liang, the new commissioner, was a much younger man than Chin. He was a fair Chinese scholar, but not a member of the Hanlin College. He was doubtless recommended by Chin Lan Pin. He brought his family with him, which consisted of his second wife and two children. He was a man of a quiet disposition and showed no inclination to meddle with settled conditions or to create trouble, but took rather a philosophical view of things; he had the good sense to let well enough alone. He was connected with the mission but a short time and resigned in 1876.

In 1876 Chin Lan Pin came as minister plenipotentiary and brought with him among his numerous retinue Woo Tsze Tung, a man whom I knew in Shanghai even in the '50's. He was a member of the Hanlin College, but for some reason or other, he was never assigned to any government department, nor was he ever known to hold any kind of government office. He showed a decided taste for chemistry, but never seemed to have made any progress in it, and was regarded by all his friends as a crank.

After Ou's resignation, Chin Lan Pin before proceeding to Washington to take up his official position as Chinese minister, strongly recommended Woo Tsze Tung to succeed Ou as commissioner, to which Viceroy Li Hung Chang acceded without thinking of the consequences to follow. From this time forth the educational mission found an enemy who was determined to undermine the work of Tsang Kwoh Fan and Ting Yih Cheong, to both of whom Woo Tsze Tung was more or less hostile. Woo was a member of the reactionary party, which looked upon the Chinese Educational Commission as a move subversive of the principles and theories of Chinese culture. This was told me by one of Chin's suite who held the appointment of *chargé d'affaires* for Peru. The making of Woo Tsze Tung a commissioner plainly revealed the fact that Chin Lan Pin himself was at heart an uncompromising Confucian and practically represented the reactionary party with all its rigid and uncompromising conservatism that gnashes its teeth against all and every attempt put forth to reform the government or to improve the general condition of things in China. This accounts for the fact that in the early stages of the mission, I had many and bitter altercations with him on many things which had to be settled for good, once and for all. Such as the *school* and *personal* expenses of the students; their vacation expenses; their change of costume; their attendance at family worship; their attendance at Sunday School and church services; their outdoor exercises and athletic games. These and other questions of a social nature came up for settlement. I had to stand as a kind of buffer between Chin and the students, and defended them in all their reasonable claims. It was in this manner that I must have incurred Chin's displeasure if not his utter dislike. He had never been out of China in his life until he came to this country. The only standard by which he measured things and men (especially students) was purely Chinese. The gradual but marked transformation of the students in their behavior and conduct as they grew in knowledge and stature under New England influence, culture and environment produced a contrast to their behavior and conduct when they first set foot in New England that might well be strange and repugnant to the ideas and senses of a man like Chin Lan Pin, who all his life had been accustomed to see the springs of life, energy and independence, candor, ingenuity and open-heartedness all covered up and concealed, and in a great measure smothered and never allowed their full play. Now in New England the heavy weight of repression and suppression was lifted from the minds of these young students; they exulted in their freedom and leaped for joy. No wonder they took to athletic sports with alacrity and delight!

Doubtless Chin Lan Pin when he left Hartford for good to go to Washington carried away with him a very poor idea of the work to which he was singled out and called upon to perform. He must have felt that his own immaculate Chinese training had been contaminated by coming in contact with Occidental schooling, which he looked upon with evident repugnance. At the same time the very work which he seemed to look upon with disgust had certainly served him the best turn in his life. It served to lift him out of his obscurity as a head clerk in the office of the Board of Punishment for twenty years to become a commissioner of the Chinese Educational Commission, and from that post to be a minister plenipotentiary in Washington. It was the stepping stone by which he climbed to political prominence. He should not have kicked away the ladder under him after he had reached his dizzy elevation. He did all he could to break up the educational scheme by recommending Woo Tsze Tung to be the Commissioner of Education, than whom he could not have had a more pliant and subservient tool for his purpose, as may be seen hereinafter.

Woo Tsze Tung was installed commissioner in the fall of 1876. No sooner was he in office than he began to find fault with everything that had been done. Instead of laying those complaints before me, he clandestinely started a stream of misrepresentation to Peking about the students; how they had been mismanaged; how they had been indulged and petted by Commissioner Yung; how they had been allowed to enjoy more privileges than was good for them; how they imitated American students in athletics; that they played more than they studied; that they formed themselves into secret societies, both religious and political; that they ignored their teachers and would not listen to the advice of the new commissioner; that if they were allowed to continue to have their own way, they would soon lose their love of their own country, and on their return to China, they would be good for nothing or worse than nothing; that most of them went to church, attended Sunday Schools and had become Christians; that the sooner this educational enterprise was broken up and all the students recalled, the better it would be for China, etc., etc.

Such malicious misrepresentations and other falsehoods which we knew nothing of, were kept up in a continuous stream from year to year by Woo Tsze Tung to his friends in Peking and to Viceroy Li Hung Chang. The Viceroy called my attention to Woo's accusations. I wrote back in reply that they were malicious fabrications of a man who was known to have been a crank all his life; that it was a grand mistake to put such a man in a responsible position who had done nothing for himself or for others in his life; that he was only attempting to destroy the work of Tsang Kwoh Fan who, by projecting and fathering the educational mission, had the highest interest of China at heart; whereas Woo should have been relegated to a cell in an insane asylum or to an institution for imbeciles. I said further that Chin Lan Pin, who had recommended Woo to His Excellency as commissioner of Chinese Education, was a timid man by nature and trembled at the sight of the smallest responsibilities. He and I had not agreed in our line of policy in our diplomatic correspondence with the State Department nor had we agreed as commissioners in regard to the treatment of the Chinese students. To illustrate his extreme dislike of responsibilities: He was requested by the Governor to go to Cuba to find out the condition of the coolies in that island in 1873. He waited three months before he started on his journey. He sent Yeh Shu Tung and one of the teachers of the Mission accompanied by a young American lawyer and an interpreter to Cuba, which party did the burden of the work and thus paved the way for Chin Lan Pin and made the work easy for him. All he had to do was to take a trip down to Cuba and return, fulfilling his mission in a perfunctory way. The heat of the day and the burden of the labor were all borne by Yeh Shu Tung, but Chin Lan Pin gathered in the laurel and was made a minister plenipotentiary, while Yeh was given the appointment of a secretary of the legation. I mention these things not from any invidious motive towards Chin, but simply to show that often in the official and political world one man gets more praise and glory than he really deserves, while another is not rewarded according to his intrinsic worth. His Excellency was well aware that I had no axe to grind in making the foregoing statement. I further added that I much preferred not to accept the appointment of a minister to Washington, but rather to remain as commissioner of education, for the sole purpose of carrying it through to its final success. And, one time in the heat of our altercation over a letter addressed to the State Department, I told Chin Lan Pin in plain language that I did not care a rap either for the appointment of an assistant minister, or for that matter, of a full minister, and that I was ready and would gladly resign at any moment, leaving him free and independent to do as he pleased.

This letter in answer to the Viceroy's note calling my attention to Woo's accusations gave the Viceroy an insight into Woo's antecedents, as well as into the impalpable character of Chin Lan Pin. Li was, of course, in the dark as to what the Viceroy had written to Chin Lan Pin, but things both in the legation and the Mission apparently moved on smoothly for a while, till some of the students were advanced enough in their studies for me to make application to the State Department for admittance to the Military Academy at West Point and the Naval Academy in Annapolis. The answer to my application was: "There is no room provided for Chinese students." It was curt and disdainful. It breathed the spirit of Kearnyism and Sandlotism with which the whole Pacific atmosphere was impregnated, and which had hypnotized all the departments of the government, especially Congress, in which Blaine figured most conspicuously as the champion against the Chinese on the floor of the Senate. He had the presidential bee buzzing in his bonnet at the time, and did his best to cater for the electoral votes of the Pacific coast. The race prejudice against the Chinese was so rampant and rank that not only my application for the students to gain entrance to Annapolis and West Point was treated with cold indifference and scornful hauteur, but the Burlingame Treaty of 1868 was, without the least provocation, and contrary to all diplomatic precedents and common decency, trampled under foot unceremoniously and wantonly, and set aside as though no such treaty had ever existed, in order to make way for those acts of congressional discrimination against Chinese immigration which were pressed for immediate enactment.

When I wrote to the Viceroy that I had met with a rebuff in my attempt to have some of the students admitted to West Point and Annapolis, his reply at once convinced me that the fate of the Mission was sealed. He too fell back on the Burlingame Treaty of 1868 to convince me that the United States government had violated the treaty by shutting out our students from West Point and Annapolis.

Having given a sketch of the progress of the Chinese Educational Mission from 1870 to 1877–8, my letter applying for their admittance into the Military and Naval Academies might be regarded as my last official act as a commissioner. My duties from 1878 onwards were chiefly confined to legation work.

When the news that my application for the students to enter the Military and Naval Academies of the government had proved a failure, and the displeasure and disappointment of the Viceroy at the rebuff were known, Commissioner Woo once more renewed his efforts to break up the Mission. This time he had the secret co-operation of Chin Lan Pin. Misrepresentations and falsehoods manufactured out of the whole cloth went forth to Peking in renewed budgets in every mail, till a censor from the ranks of the reactionary party came forward and took advantage of the strong anti-Chinese prejudices in America to memorialize the government to break up the Mission and have all the students recalled.

The government before acceding to the memorial put the question to Viceroy Li Hung Chang first, who, instead of standing up for the students, yielded to the opposition of the reactionary party and gave his assent to have the students recalled. Chin Lan Pin, who from his personal experience was supposed to know what ought to be done, was the next man asked to give his opinion. He decided that the students had been in the United States long enough, and that it was time for them to return to China. Woo Tsze Tung, the Commissioner, when asked for his opinion, came out point blank and said that they should be recalled without delay and should be strictly watched after their return. I was ruled out of the consultation altogether as being one utterly incompetent to give an impartial and reliable opinion on the subject. Thus the fate of the educational mission was sealed, and all students, about one hundred in all, returned to China in 1881.

The breaking up of the Chinese Educational Commission and the recall of the young students in 1881, was not brought about without a strenuous effort on the part of some thoughtful men who had watched steadfastly over the development of human progress in the East and the West, who came forward in their quiet and modest ways to enter a protest against the revocation of the Mission. Chief among them were my lifelong friend, the Rev. J. H. Twichell, and Rev. John W. Lane, through whose persistent efforts Presidents Porter and Seelye, Samuel Clemens, T. F. Frelinghuysen, John Russell Young and others were enlisted and brought forward to stay the work of retrogression of the part of the Chinese. The protest was couched in the most dignified, frank and manly language of President Porter of Yale and read as follows:

To The Tsung Li Yamun
or
Office for Foreign Affairs.

"The undersigned, who have been instructors, guardians and friends of the students who were sent to this country under the care of the Chinese Educational Commission, beg leave to represent:

"That they exceedingly regret that these young men have been withdrawn from the country, and that the Educational Commission has been dissolved.

"So far as we have had opportunity to observe, and can learn from the representations of others, the young men have generally made a faithful use of their opportunities, and have made good progress in the studies assigned to them, and in the knowledge of the language, ideas, arts and institutions of the people of this country.

"With scarcely a single exception, their morals have been good; their manners have been singularly polite and decorous, and their behavior has been such as to make friends for themselves and their country in the families, the schools, the cities and villages in which they have resided.

"In these ways they have proved themselves eminently worthy of the confidence which has been reposed in them to represent their families and the great Chinese Empire in a land of strangers. Though children and youths, they have seemed always to understand that the honor of their race and their nation was committed to their keeping. As the result of their good conduct, many of the prejudices of ignorant and wicked men towards the Chinese have been removed, and more favorable sentiments have taken their place.

"We deeply regret that the young men have been taken away just at the time when they were about to reap the most important advantages from their previous studies, and to gather in the rich harvest which their painful and laborious industry had been preparing for them to reap. The studies which most of them have pursued hitherto have been disciplinary and preparatory. The studies of which they have been deprived by their removal, would have been the bright flower and the ripened fruit of the roots and stems which have been slowly reared under patient watering and tillage. We have given to them the same knowledge and culture that we give to our own children and citizens.

"As instructors and guardians of these young men, we should have welcomed to our schools and colleges the Commissioners of Education or their representatives and have explained to them our system and methods of instruction. In some cases, they have been invited to visit us, but have failed to respond to their invitations in person or by their deputies.

"We would remind your honorable body that these students were originally received to our homes and our colleges by request of the Chinese government through the Secretary of State with the express desire that they might learn our language, our manners, our sciences and our arts. To remove them permanently and suddenly without formal notice or inquiry on the ground that as yet they had learned nothing useful to China when their education in Western institutions, arts and sciences is as yet incomplete, seems to us as unworthy of the great Empire for which we wish eminent prosperity and peace, as it is discourteous to the nation that extended to these young men its friendly hospitality.

"We cannot accept as true the representation that they have derived evil and not good from our institutions, our principles and our manners. If they have neglected or forgotten their native language, we never assumed the duty of instructing them in it, and cannot be held responsible for this neglect. The Chinese government thought it wise that some of its own youth should be trained after our methods. We have not finished the work which we were expected to perform. May we not reasonably be displeased that the results of our work should be judged unfavorably before it could possibly be finished?

"In view of these considerations, and especially in view of the injury and loss which have fallen upon the young men whom we have learned to respect and love, and the reproach which has implicitly been brought upon ourselves and the great nation to which we belong,—we would respectfully urge that the reasons for this sudden decision should be reconsidered, and the representations which have been made concerning the intellectual and moral character of our education should be properly substantiated. We would suggest that to this end, a committee may be appointed of eminent Chinese citizens whose duty it shall be to examine into the truth of the statements unfavorable to the young men or their teachers, which have led to the unexpected abandonment of the Educational Commission and to the withdrawal of the young men from the United States before their education could be finished."

XX

JOURNEY TO PEKING AND DEATH OF MY WIFE

The treatment which the students received at the hands of Chinese officials in the first years after their return to China as compared with the treatment they received in America while at school could not fail to make an impression upon their innermost convictions of the superiority of Occidental civilization over that of China—an impression which will always appeal to them as cogent and valid ground for radical reforms in China, however altered their conditions may be in their subsequent careers. Quite a number of the survivors of the one hundred students, I am happy to say, have risen to high official ranks and positions of great trust and responsibility. The eyes of the government have been opened to see the grand mistake it made in breaking up the Mission and having the students recalled. Within only a few years it had the candor and magnanimity to confess that it wished it had more of just such men as had been turned out by the Chinese Educational Mission in Hartford, Conn. This confession, though coming too late, may be taken as a sure sign that China is really awakening and is making the best use of what few partially educated men are available. And these few Occidentally educated men have, in their turn, encouraged and stimulated both the government and the people. Since the memorable events of the China and Japan war, and the war between Japan and Russia, several hundreds of Chinese students have come over to the United States to be educated. Thus the Chinese educational scheme which Tsang Kwoh Fan initiated in 1870 at Tientsin and established in Hartford, Conn., in 1872, though rolled back for a period of twenty-five years, has been practically revived.

Soon after the students' recall and return to China in 1881, I also took my departure and arrived in Tientsin in the fall of that year on my way to Peking to report myself to the government after my term of office as assistant minister had expired. This was the customary step for all diplomatic officers of the government to take at the close of their terms. Chin Lan Pin preceded me by nearly a year, having returned in 1880.

While paying my visit to Li Hung Chang in Tientsin, before going up to Peking, he brought up the subject of the recall of the students. To my great astonishment he asked me why I had allowed the students to return to China. Not knowing exactly the significance of the inquiry, I said that Chin Lan Pin, who was minister, had received an imperial decree to break up the Mission; that His Excellency was in favor of the decree, so was Chin Lan Pin and so was Woo Tsze Tung. If I had stood out alone against carrying out the imperial mandate, would not I have been regarded as a rebel, guilty of treason, and lose my head for it? But he said that at heart he was in favor of their being kept in the States to continue their studies, and that I ought to have detained them. In reply I asked how I could have been supposed to read his heart at a distance of 45,000 lis, especially when it was well known that His Excellency had said that they might just as well be recalled. If His Excellency had written to me beforehand not to break up the Mission under any circumstances, I would then have known what to do; as it was, I could not have done otherwise than to see the decree carried out. "Well," said he, in a somewhat angry and excited tone, "I know the author of this great mischief." Woo Tsze Tung happened to be in Tientsin at the time. He had just been to Peking and sent me word begging me to call and see him. Out of courtesy, I did call. He told me he had not been well received in Peking, and that Viceroy Li was bitter towards him when he had called and had refused to see him a second time. He looked careworn and cast down. He was never heard of after our last interview.

On my arrival in Peking, one of my first duties was to make my round of official calls on the leading dignitaries of the government—the Princes Kung and Ching and the presidents of the six boards. It took me nearly a month to finish these official calls. Peking may be said to be a city of great distances, and the high officials live quite far apart from each other. The only conveyances that were used to go about from place to place were the mule carts. These were heavy, clumsy vehicles with an axle-tree running right across under the body of a box, which was the carriage, and without springs to break the jolting, with two heavy wheels, one at each end of the axle. They were slow coaches, and with the Peking roads all cut up and seldom repaired, you can imagine what traveling in those days meant. The dust and smell of the roads were something fearful. The dust was nothing but pulverized manure almost as black as ink. It was ground so fine by the millions of mule carts that this black stuff would fill one's eyes and ears and penetrate deep into the pores of one's skin, making it impossible to cleanse oneself with one washing. The neck, head and hands had to have suitable coverings to keep off the dust. The water is brackish, making it difficult to take off the dirt, thereby adding to the discomforts of living in Peking.

I was in Peking about three months. While there, I found time to prepare a plan for the effectual suppression of the Indian opium trade in China and the extinction of the poppy cultivation in China and India. This plan was submitted to the Chinese government to be carried out, but I was told by Whang Wen Shiu, the president of the Tsung Li Yamun (Foreign Affairs), that for want of suitable men, the plan could not be entertained, and it was shelved for nearly a quarter of a century until recently when the subject became an international question.

I left Peking in 1882. After four months' residence in Shanghai, I returned to the United States on account of the health of my family.

I reached home in the spring of 1883, and found my wife in a very low condition. She had lost the use of her voice and greeted me in a hoarse low whisper. I was thankful that I found her still living though much emaciated. In less than a month after my return, she began to pick up and felt more like herself. Doubtless, her declining health and suffering were brought on partly on account of my absence and her inexpressible anxiety over the safety of my life. A missionary fresh from China happened to call on her a few days before my departure for China and told her that my going back to China was a hazardous step, as they would probably cut my head off on account of the Chinese Educational Mission. This piece of gratuitous information tended more to aggravate a mind already weighed down by poor health, and to have this gloomy foreboding added to her anxiety was more than she could bear. I was absent in China from my family this time nearly a year and a half, and I made up my mind that I would never leave it again under any conditions whatever. My return in 1883 seemed to act on my wife's health and spirit like magic, as she gradually recovered strength enough to go up to Norfolk for the summer. The air up in Norfolk was comparatively pure and more wholesome than in the Connecticut valley, and proved highly salubrious to her condition. At the close of the summer, she came back a different person from what she was when she went away, and I was much encouraged by her improved health. I followed up these changes of climate and air with the view of restoring her to her normal condition, taking her down to Atlanta, Georgia, one winter and to the Adirondacks another year. It seemed that these changes brought only temporary relief without any permanent recovery. In the winter of 1885, she began to show signs of a loss of appetite and expressed a desire for a change. Somerville, New Jersey, was recommended to her as a sanitarium. That was the last resort she went to for her health, for there she caught a cold which resulted in her death. She lingered there for nearly two months till she was brought home, and died of Bright's disease on the 28th of June, 1886. She was buried in Cedar Hill Cemetery in the home lot I secured for that purpose. Her death made a great void in my after-life, which was irreparable, but she did not leave me hopelessly deserted and alone; she left me two sons who are constant reminders of her beautiful life and character. They have proved to be my greatest comfort and solace in my declining years. They are most faithful, thoughtful and affectionate sons, and I am proud of their manly and earnest Christian characters. My gratitude to God for blessing me with two such sons will forever rise to heaven, an endless incense.

The two blows that fell upon me one after the other within the short span of five years from 1880 to 1886 were enough to crush my spirit. The one had scattered my life work to the four winds; the other had deprived me of a happy home which had lasted only ten years. The only gleam of light that broke through the dark clouds which hung over my head came from my two motherless sons whose tender years appealed to the very depths of my soul for care and sympathy. They were respectively seven and nine years old when deprived of their mother. I was both father and mother to them from 1886 till 1895. My whole soul was wrapped up in their education and well-being. My mother-in-law, Mrs. Mary B. Kellogg, assisted me in my work and stood by me in my most trying hours, keeping house for me for nearly two years.

XXI

MY RECALL TO CHINA

In 1894–5 war broke out between China and Japan on account of Korea. My sympathies were enlisted on the side of China, not because I am a Chinese, but because China had the right on her side, and Japan was simply trumping up a pretext to go to war with China, in order to show her military and naval prowess. Before the close of the war, it was impossible for me to be indifferent to the situation—I could not repress my love for China. I wrote to my former legation interpreter and secretary, two letters setting forth a plan by which China might prosecute the war for an indefinite time.

My first plan was to go over to London to negotiate a loan of $15,000,000, with which sum to purchase three or four ready built iron-clads, to raise a foreign force of 5,000 men to attack Japan in the rear from the Pacific coast—thus creating a diversion to draw the Japanese forces from Korea and give the Chinese government a breathing spell to recruit a fresh army and a new navy to cope with Japan. While this plan was being carried out, the government was to empower a commission to mortgage the Island of Formosa to some Western power for the sum of $400,000,000 for the purpose of organizing a national army and navy to carry on the war. These plans were embodied in two letters to Tsai Sik Yung, at that time secretary to Chang Tsze Tung, viceroy of Hunan and Hupeh. They were translated into Chinese for the Viceroy. That was in the winter of 1894. To my great surprise, Viceroy Chang approved of my first plan. I was authorized by cable to go over to London to negotiate the loan of $15,000,000. The Chinese minister in London, a Li Hung Chang man, was advised of my mission, which in itself was a sufficient credential for me to present myself to the minister. In less than a month after my arrival in London, I succeeded in negotiating the loan; but in order to furnish collaterals for it, I had to get the Chinese minister in London to cable the government for the hypothecation of the customs' revenue. I was told that Sir Robert Hart, inspector-general of customs, and Viceroy Li Hung Chang refused to have the customs' revenue hypothecated, on the ground that this revenue was hardly enough to cover as collateral the loan to meet the heavy indemnity demanded by

Japan. The fact was: Viceroy Li Hung Chang and Chang Chi Tung were at loggerheads and opposed to each other in the conduct of the war. The latter was opposed to peace being negotiated by Li Hung Chang; but the former had the Dowager Empress on his side and was strenuous in his efforts for peace.

Hence Sir Robert Hart had to side with the Court party, and ignored Chang Chi Tung's request for the loan of $15,000,000; on that account the loan fell through, and came near involving me in a suit with the London Banking Syndicate.

I returned to New York and cabled for further instructions from Chang Chi Tung as to what my next step would be. In reply he cabled for me to come to China at once.

After thirteen years of absence from China, I thought that my connections with the Chinese government had been severed for good when I left there in 1883. But it did not appear to be so; another call to return awaited me, this time from a man whom I had never seen, of whose character, disposition and views I was altogether ignorant, except from what I knew from hearsay. But he seemed to know all about me, and in his memorial to the government inviting me to return, he could not have spoken of me in higher terms than he did. So I girded myself to go back once more to see what there was in store for me. By this recall, I became Chang Chi Tung's man as opposed to Li Hung Chang.

Before leaving for China this time, I took special pains to see my two sons well provided for in their education. Dr. E. W. Kellogg, my oldest brother-in-law, was appointed their guardian. Morrison Brown Yung, the older son, had just succeeded in entering Yale, Sheffield Scientific, and was able to look out for himself. Bartlett G. Yung, the younger one, was still in the Hartford High School preparing for college. I was anxious to secure a good home for him before leaving the country, as I did not wish to leave him to shift for himself at his critical age. The subject was mentioned to my friends, Mr. and Mrs. Twichell. They at once came forward and proposed to take Bartlett into their family as one of its members, till he was ready to enter college. This is only a single instance illustrative of the large-hearted and broad spirit which has endeared them to their people both in the Asylum Hill church and outside of it. I was deeply affected by this act of self-denial and magnanimity in my behalf as well as in the behalf of my son Bartlett, whom I felt perfectly assured was in first-class hands, adopted as a member of one of the best families in New England. Knowing that my sons would be well cared for, and leaving the development of their characters to an all-wise and ever-ruling Providence, as well as to their innate qualities, I embarked for China, this time without any definite and specific object in view beyond looking out for what opening there might be for me to serve her.

On my arrival in Shanghai, in the early part of the summer of 1895, I had to go to the expense of furnishing myself with a complete outfit of all my official dresses, which cost me quite a sum. Viceroy Chang Chi Tung, a short time previous to my arrival, had been transferred from the viceroyalty of the two Hoos to the viceroyalty of the two Kiangs temporarily. Instead of going up to Wu Chang, the capital of Hupeh, I went up to Nanking, where he was quartered.

In Viceroy Chang Chi Tung, I did not find that magnetic attraction which at once drew me towards Tsang Kwoh Fan when I first met him at Ngan Khing in 1863. There was a cold, supercilious air enveloping him, which at once put me on my guard. After stating in a summary way how the loan of $15,000,000 fell through, he did not state why the Peking government had declined to endorse his action in authorizing the loan, though I knew at the time that Sir Robert Hart, the inspector-general of the Chinese customs, put forward as an excuse that the custom dues were hardly enough to serve as collateral for the big loan that was about to be negotiated to satisfy the war indemnity demanded by the Japanese government. This was the diplomatic way of coating over a bitter pill for Chang Chi Tung to swallow, when the Peking government, through the influence of Li Hung Chang, was induced to ignore the loan. Chang and Li were not at the time on cordial terms, each having a divergent policy to follow in regard to the conduct of the war.

Dropping the subject of the loan as a dead issue, our next topic of conversation was the political state of the country in view of the humiliating defeat China had suffered through the incompetence and corruption of Li Hung Chang, whose defeat both on land and sea had stripped him of all official rank and title and came near costing him his life. I said that China, in order to recover her prestige and become a strong and powerful nation, would have to adopt a new policy. She would have to go to work and engage at least four foreigners to act as advisers in the Department for Foreign Affairs, in the Military and Naval Departments and in the Treasury Department. They might be engaged for a period of ten years, at the end of which time they might be re-engaged for another term. They would have to be men of practical experience, of unquestioned ability and character. While these men were thus engaged to give their best advice in their respective departments, it should be taken up and acted upon, and young and able Chinese students should be selected to work under them. In that way, the government would have been rebuilt upon Western methods, and on principles and ideas that look to the reformation of the administrative government of China.

Such was the sum and substance of my talk in the first and only interview with which Chang Chi Tung favored me. During the whole of it, he did not express his opinion at all on any of the topics touched upon. He was as reticent and absorbent as a dry sponge. The interview differed from that accorded me by Tsang Kwoh Fan in 1863, in that Tsang had already made up his mind what he wanted to do for China, and I was pointed out to him to execute it. But in the case of Chang Chi Tung, he had no plan formed for China at the time, and what I presented to him in the interview was entirely new and somewhat radical; but the close of the Japan War justified me in bringing forward such views, as it was on account of that war that I had been recalled. If he had been as broad a statesman as his predecessor, Tsang Kwoh Fan, he could have said something to encourage me to entertain even a glimpse of hope that he was going to do something to reform the political condition of the government of the country at the close of the war. Nothing, however, was said, or even hinted at. In fact, I had no other interview with him after the first one. Before he left Nanking for Wu Chang, he gave me the appointment of Secretary of Foreign Affairs for Kiang Nan.

On the arrival of Liu Kwan Yih, the permanent viceroy of the two Kiang provinces, Chang Chi Tung did not ask me to go up to Wu Chang with him. This I took to be a pretty broad hint that he did not need my services any longer, that I was not the man to suit his purposes; and as I had no axe to grind, I did not make any attempt to run after my grind-stone. On the contrary, after three months' stay in Nanking under Viceroy Liu Kwan Yih, out of regard for official etiquette, I resigned the secretaryship, which was practically a sinecure—paying about $150 a month. Such was my brief official experience with Viceroys Chang Chi Tung and Liu Kwan Yih.

I severed my official connection with the provincial government of Kiang Nan in 1896, and took up my headquarters in Shanghai—

untrammeled and free to do as I pleased and go where I liked. It was then that I conceived the plan of inducing the central government to establish in Peking a government national bank. For this object I set to work translating into Chinese the National Banking Act and other laws relating to national banks from the Revised Statutes of the United States with Amendments and additional Acts of 1875. In prosecuting this work, I had the aid of a Chinese writer, likewise the co-operation of the late Wong Kai Keh, one of the Chinese students who was afterwards the assistant Chinese commissioner in the St. Louis Exposition, who gave me valuable help. With the translation, I went up to Peking with my Chinese writer, and, at the invitation of my old friend, Chang Yen Hwan, who had been Chinese Minister in Washington from 1884 to 1888, I took up my quarters in his residence and remained there several months. Chang Yen Hwan at that time held two offices: one as a senior member of the Tsung Li Yamun (Office for Foreign Affairs); the other, as the first secretary in the Treasury Department of which Ung Tung Hwo, tutor to the late Emperor Kwang Su, was the president. Chang Yen Hwan was greatly interested in the National Banking scheme. He examined the translation critically and suggested that I should leave out those articles that were inapplicable to the conditions of China, and retain only such as were important and practicable. After the translation and selection were completed, he showed it to Ung Tung Hwo, president of the Treasury. They were both highly pleased with it, and had all the Treasury officials look it over carefully and pass their judgment upon it. In a few weeks' time, the leading officials of the Treasury Department called upon me to congratulate me upon my work, and said it ought to be made a subject of a memorial to the government to have the banking scheme adopted and carried out. Chang Yen Hwan came forward to champion it, backed by Ung Tung Hwo, the president.

To have a basis upon which to start the National Bank of China, it was necessary to have the government advance the sum of Tls. 10,000,000; of this sum, upwards of Tls. 2,000,000 were to be spent on machinery for printing government bonds and bank-notes of different denominations and machinery for a mint; Tls. 2,000,000 for the purchase of land and buildings; and Tls. 6,000,000 were to be held in reserve in the Treasury for the purchase of gold, silver and copper for minting coins of different denominations for general circulation. This Tls. 10,000,000 was to be taken as the initiatory sum to start the

National Bank with, and was to be increased every year in proportion to the increase of the commerce of the Empire.

We had made such progress in our project as to warrant our appointing a committee to go around to select a site for the Bank, while I was appointed to come to the United States to consult with the Treasury Department on the plan and scope of the enterprise and to learn the best course to take in carrying out the plan of the National Bank. The Treasury Department, through its president, Ung Tung Hwo, was on the point of memorializing for an imperial decree to sanction setting aside the sum of Tls. 10,000,000 for the purpose indicated, when, to the astonishment of Chang Yen Hwan and other promoters of the enterprise, Ung Tung Hwo, the president, received a telegraphic message from Shing Sun Whei, head of the Chinese Telegraphic Co., and manager of the Shanghai, China Steamship Navigation Co., asking Ung to suspend his action for a couple of weeks, till his arrival in Peking, Ung and Shing being intimate friends, besides being compatriots, Ung acceded to Shing's request. Shing Taotai, as he was called, was well-known to be a multimillionaire, and no great enterprise or concession of any kind could pass through without his finger in the pie. So in this banking scheme, he was bound to have his say. He had emissaries all over Peking who kept him well posted about everything going on in the capital as well as outside of it. He had access to the most powerful and influential princes in Peking, his system of graft reaching even the Dowager Empress through her favorite eunuch, the notorious Li Ling Ying. So Shing was a well-known character in Chinese politics. It was through his system of graft that the banking enterprise was defeated. It was reported that he came up to Peking with Tls. 300,000 as presents to two or three princes and other high and influential dignitaries, and got away with the Tls. 10,000,000 of appropriation by setting up a bank to manipulate his own projects.

The defeat of the National Banking project owed its origin to the thoroughly corrupt condition of the administrative system of China. From the Dowager Empress down to the lowest and most petty underling in the Empire, the whole political fabric was honey-combed with what Americans characterize as graft—a species of political barnacles, if I may be allowed to call it that, which, when once allowed to fasten their hold upon the bottom of the ship of State were sure to work havoc and ruination; in other words, with money one could get anything done in China. Everything was for barter; the highest bid got the prize. The two wars—the one with Japan in 1894–5 and the other, the Japan and Russian War in 1904–5—have in some measure purified the Eastern atmosphere, and the Chinese have finally awakened to their senses and have come to some sane consciousness of their actual condition.

After the defeat of the national banking project at the hands of Shing Taotai, I went right to work to secure a railroad concession from the government. The railroad I had in mind was one between the two ports of Tientsin and Chinkiang; one in the north, the other in the south near the mouth of the Yangtze River. The distance between these ports in a bee line is about five hundred miles; by a circuitous route going around the province of Shan Tung and crossing the Yellow River into the province of Hunan through Anwhui, the distance would be about seven hundred miles. The German government objected to having this railroad cross Shan Tung province, as they claimed they had the monopoly of building railroads throughout the province, and would not allow another party to build a railroad across Shan Tung. This was a preposterous and absurd pretension and could not be supported either by the international laws or the sovereign laws of China. At that time, China was too feeble and weak to take up the question and assert her own sovereign rights in the matter, nor had she the men in the Foreign Office to show up the absurdity of the pretension. So, to avoid any international complications, the concession was issued to me with the distinct understanding that the road was to be built by the circuitous route above described. The road was to be built with Chinese, not with foreign capital. I was given six months' time to secure capital. At the end of six months, if I failed to show capital, I was to surrender the concession. I knew very well that it would be impossible to get Chinese capitalists to build any railroad at that time. I tried hard to get around the sticking point by getting foreign syndicates to take over the concession, but all my attempts proved abortive, and I was compelled to give up my railroad scheme also. This ended my last effort to help China.

I did not dream that in the midst of my work, Khang Yu Wei and his disciple, Leang Kai Chiu, whom I met often in Peking during the previous year, were engaged in the great work of reform which was soon to culminate in the momentous *coup d'état* of 1898.

XXII

The Coup D'etat of 1898

The *coup d'état* of September, 1898, was an event memorable in the annals of the Manchu Dynasty. In it, the late Emperor Kwang Su was arbitrarily deposed; treasonably made a prisoner of state; and had his prerogatives and rights as Emperor of the Chinese Empire wrested from him and usurped by the late Dowager Empress Chi Hsi.

Kwang Su, though crowned Emperor when he was five years of age, had all along held the sceptre only nominally. It was Chi Hsi who held the helm of the government all the time.

As soon as Kwang Su had attained his majority, and began to exercise his authority as emperor, the lynx eye of Chi Hsi was never lifted away from him. His acts and movements were watched with the closest scrutiny, and were looked upon in any light but the right one, because her own stand in the government had never been the legitimate and straight one since 1864, when her first regency over her own son, Tung Chi, woke in her an ambition to dominate and rule, which grew to be a passion too morbid and strong to be curbed.

In the assertion of his true manhood, and the exercise of his sovereign power, his determination to reform the government made him at once the cynosure of Peking, inside and outside of the Palace. In the eyes of the Dowager Empress Chi Hsi, whose retina was darkened by deeds perpetrated in the interest of usurpation and blinded by jealousy, Kwang Su appeared in no other light than as a dement, or to use a milder expression, an imbecile, fit only to be tagged round by an apron string, cared for and watched. But to the disinterested spectator and unprejudiced judge, Kwan Su was no imbecile, much less a dement. Impartial history and posterity will pronounce him not only a patriot emperor, but also a patriot reformer—as mentally sound and sane as any emperor who ever sat on the throne of China. He may be looked upon as a most remarkable historical character of the Manchu Dynasty from the fact that he was singled out by an all-wise Providence to be the pioneer of the great reform movement in China at the threshold of the twentieth century.

Just at this juncture of the political condition of China, the tide of reform had reached Peking. Emperor Kwang Su, under some mysterious influence, to the astonishment of the world, stood forth as the exponent of this reform movement. I determined to remain in the city to watch its progress. My headquarters became the rendez-vous of the leading reformers of 1898. It was in the fall of that memorable year that the *coup d'état* took place, in which the young Emperor Kwang Su was deposed by the Dowager Empress, and some of the leading reformers arrested and summarily decapitated.

Being implicated by harboring the reformers, and in deep sympathy with them, I had to flee for my own life and succeeded in escaping from Peking. I took up quarters in the foreign settlement of Shanghai. While there, I organized the "Deliberative Association of China," of which I was chosen the first president. The object of the association was to discuss the leading question of the day, especially those of reform.

In 1899, I was advised for my own personal safety, to change my residence. I went to Hong Kong and placed myself under the protection of the British government.

I was in Hong Kong from 1900 till 1902, when I returned to the United States to see my younger son, Bartlett G. Yung, graduate from Yale University.

In the spring of 1901, I visited the Island of Formosa, and in that visit I called upon Viscount Gentaro Kodama, governor of the island, who, in the Russo-Japan War of 1904–5 was the chief of staff to Marshal Oyama in Manchuria. In the interview our conversation had to be carried on through his interpreter, as he, Kodama, could not speak English nor could I speak Japanese.

He said he was glad to see me, as he had heard a great deal of me, but never had the pleasure of meeting me. Now that he had the opportunity, he said he might as well tell me that he had most unpleasant if not painful information to give me. Being somewhat surprised at such an announcement, I asked what the information was. He said he had received from the viceroy of Fuhkein and Chêhkiang an official despatch requesting him to have me arrested, if found in Formosa, and sent over to the mainland to be delivered over to the Chinese authorities. Kodama while giving this information showed neither perturbation of thought nor feeling, but his whole countenance was wreathed with a calm and even playful smile.

I was not disturbed by this unexpected news, nor was I at all excited. I met it calmly and squarely, and said in reply that I was entirely in his power, that he could deliver me over to my enemies whenever he wished; I was ready to die for China at any time, provided that the death was an honorable one.

"Well, Mr. Yung," said he, "I am not going to play the part of a constable for China, so you may rest at ease on this point. I shall not deliver you over to China. But I have another matter to call to your attention." I asked what it was. He immediately held up a Chinese newspaper before me, and asked who was the author of the proposition. Without the least hesitation. I told him I was the author of it. At the same time, to give emphasis to this open declaration, I put my opened right palm on my chest two or three times, which attracted the attention of everyone in the room, and caused a slight excitement among the Japanese officials present.

I then said, "With Your Excellency's permission, I must beg to make one correction in the amount stated; instead of $800,000,000, the sum stated in my proposition was only $400,000,000." At this frank and open declaration and the corrected sum, Kodama was evidently pleased and visibly showed his pleasure by smiling at me.

The Chinese newspaper Kodama showed me contained a proposition I drew up for Viceroy Chang Chi Tung to memorialize the Peking government for adoption in 1894–5, about six months before the signing of the Treaty of Shemonashiki by Viceroy Li Hung Chang. The proposal was to have the Island of Formosa mortgaged to a European Treaty power for a period of ninety-nine years for the sum of $400,000,000 in gold. With this sum China was to carry on the war with Japan by raising a new army and a new navy. This proposition was never carried through, but was made public in the Chinese newspapers, and a copy of it found its way to Kodama's office, where, strange to say, I was confronted with it, and I had the moral courage not only to avow its authorship but also a correction of the amount the island was to be mortgaged for.

To bring the interview to a climax, I said, should like circumstances ever arise, nothing would deter me from repeating the same proposition in order to fight Japan.

This interview with the Japanese governor of Formosa was one of the most memorable ones in my life. I thought at first that at the request of the Chinese viceroy I was going to be surrendered, and that my fate was sealed; but no sooner had the twinkling smile of Kodama lighted his countenance than my assurance of life and safety came back with redoubled strength, and I was emboldened to talk war on

Japan with perfect impunity. The bold and open stand I took on that occasion won the admiration of the governor who then invited me to accompany him to Japan where he expected to go soon to be promoted. He said he would introduce me to the Japanese emperor and other leading men of the nation. I thanked him heartily for his kindness and invitation and said I would accept such a generous invitation and consider it a great honor to accompany him on his contemplated journey, but my health would not allow me to take advantage of it. I had the asthma badly at the time.

Then, before parting, he said that my life was in danger, and that while I was in Formosa under his jurisdiction he would see that I was well protected and said that he would furnish me with a bodyguard to prevent all possibilities of assassination. So the next day he sent me four Japanese guards to watch over me at night in my quarters; and in the daytime whenever I went out, two guards would go in advance of me and two behind my jinrickisha to see that I was safe. This protection was continued for the few days I spent in Formosa till I embarked for Hong Kong. I went in person to thank the governor and to express my great obligation and gratitude to him for the deep interest he had manifested towards me.

A Note About the Author

Yung Wing (1828–1912) was an influential social and political figure in China and the United States. Born near Macau, Wing attended missionary schools before traveling west to study at more prominent American institutions. In 1854 he graduated from Yale University, becoming their first alumni of Chinese descent. He became a strong proponent of education, creating programs that would allow more children to be taught in the U.S. Wing also aided the government by brokering various business transactions between the two countries.

A Note from the Publisher

Spanning many genres, from non-fiction essays to literature classics to children's books and lyric poetry, Mint Edition books showcase the master works of our time in a modern new package. The text is freshly typeset, is clean and easy to read, and features a new note about the author in each volume. Many books also include exclusive new introductory material. Every book boasts a striking new cover, which makes it as appropriate for collecting as it is for gift giving. Mint Edition books are only printed when a reader orders them, so natural resources are not wasted. We're proud that our books are never manufactured in excess and exist only in the exact quantity they need to be read and enjoyed.

Discover more of your favorite classics with Bookfinity™.

- Track your reading with custom book lists.
- Get great book recommendations for your personalized Reader Type.
- Add reviews for your favorite books.
- AND MUCH MORE!

Visit **bookfinity.com** and take the fun Reader Type quiz to get started.

Enjoy our classic and modern companion pairings!

Printed in the USA
CPSIA information can be obtained
at www.ICGtesting.com
JSHW082359140824
68134JS00020B/2159